365

Easy
Chicken
Recipes

SWEETWATER
PRESS

365 Easy Chicken Recipes

Copyright © 2008 by Cliff Road Books

Produced by arrangement with Sweetwater Press

Printed in the United States of America

ISBN-13: 978-1-58173-729-5
ISBN-10: 1-58173-729-7

Design by Miles G. Parsons

365
Easy
Chicken
Recipes

A Recipe for Every Day of the Year

Nicole Phillips

SWEETWATER
PRESS

Table of Contents

INTRODUCTION

The value of a great, home-cooked meal can never be overestimated. Unfortunately, in these times of instant gratification, fast food and take-out too often replace home cooking. It seems that preparing a meal is just too much trouble for most people. *365 Easy Chicken Recipes* was created with these folks in mind.

For those who like to make simple, inexpensive, yet delicious meals, *365 Easy Chicken Recipes* is an indispensable resource. While the recipes in this volume were designed for the home cook's greatest ease, they are not lacking in taste or sophistication. The collection features unique dishes from around the globe, including Chicken Curry, Moo Goo Gai Pan, Chicken Quesadillas, Paella à la Valenciana, Chicken Parmesan, and dozens more. Classic American fare and comfort foods, such as Chicken and Dumplings and Chicken Pot Pie, are incorporated as well. Gourmets will have no trouble finding recipes in this book to satisfy their highly developed palates, and novice chefs will be relieved by its simple instructions and quick preparation times.

With *365 Easy Chicken Recipes*, great cooking can be enjoyed every night of the week with few ingredients and minimal effort. For delicious, straightforward, hassle-free recipes, you need not look further than this collection.

Nicole Phillips

APPETIZERS

Anchovy, Chicken, and Tomato Canapés

10 slices French-style bread, ¼-inch thick
Mayonnaise
20 anchovy filets
10 pieces pimento, cut to fit toast
4 tablespoons tomato sauce
Dash cayenne pepper
4 tablespoons finely chopped boiled chicken
Fresh parsley, chopped

Toast bread slices in a 450° oven for 5 minutes. Spread them with mayonnaise. Top with anchovy. Spread on another layer of mayonnaise and cover with a piece of pimento. Mix tomato sauce with cayenne. Spread 1 teaspoon of tomato sauce on each canapé, sprinkle with chicken, and garnish with parsley. Makes 10 servings.

Appetizer Chicken Kabobs

¾ cup soy sauce
¼ cup brown sugar
1 tablespoon vegetable oil
¼ teaspoon garlic powder
½ teaspoon ground ginger
2 boneless, skinless chicken breasts, cut into 1-inch pieces
6 green onions, cut into 1-inch pieces
1 (8-ounce) package fresh mushrooms, stems removed

Stir together first 5 ingredients and pour into a large resealable plastic bag. Add chicken, onions, and mushrooms. Marinate for 30 minutes. On metal skewers, thread chicken, onions, and mushrooms. Place on a broiler rack and broil for 3 minutes. Turn and broil another 3 minutes, or until chicken is done. Makes 4 servings.

Apple Chicken Quesadillas

2 medium tart apples, sliced
1 cup cooked, diced chicken breast
½ cup shredded fat-free Cheddar cheese
½ cup shredded part-skim mozzarella cheese
½ cup fresh or frozen corn, thawed if frozen
½ cup chopped fresh tomatoes
½ cup chopped onion
¼ teaspoon salt
6 (8-inch) flour tortillas
¾ cup shredded lettuce
¾ cup salsa
6 tablespoons fat-free sour cream

In a bowl, combine the first 8 ingredients. Place about ¼ cup on half of each tortilla. Fold tortilla in half over filling and secure with toothpicks. Place on a baking sheet coated with nonstick cooking spray. Bake at 400° for 8 to 10 minutes or until golden brown. Carefully turn quesadillas over; bake 5 to 8 minutes longer or until golden. Discard toothpicks. Cut each quesadilla into three wedges; serve with lettuce, salsa, and sour cream. Makes 18 servings.

Asian Lettuce Wraps

1 pound ground chicken
1 tablespoon light soy sauce
1 teaspoon minced garlic
2 teaspoons minced fresh ginger
1 cup brown rice
2 cups water
16 large lettuce leaves
1 cup shredded carrots
1 cup thinly sliced green onion
1 cup sliced radish
1 cup sliced red bell pepper
⅓ cup light soy sauce
⅓ cup water
3 tablespoons fresh lemon juice
2 teaspoons minced garlic
1 tablespoon minced fresh ginger
1 teaspoon sugar

In a medium bowl, mix together ground chicken, 1 tablespoon soy sauce, 1 teaspoon garlic, and 2 teaspoons ginger. Form into 16 meatballs and roll into ovals. Cover and refrigerate. In a medium saucepan over medium heat, combine rice with 2 cups water. Bring to a boil, reduce heat, and simmer for 20 minutes, or until rice is tender.

Arrange rice, lettuce leaves, carrot, green onion, radish, and red pepper onto a serving platter, or place each into a small bowl. In a medium bowl, mix together ⅓ cup soy sauce, ⅓ cup water, lemon juice, 2 teaspoons garlic, 1 tablespoon ginger, and sugar. Divide into 4 small dipping bowls. Thread meatballs onto thin 10-inch skewers. Grill or broil for 10 to 12 minutes, turning occasionally to brown all sides. If broiling, line the broiler pan with aluminum foil, and drain fat after 6 minutes.

To eat, place a leaf of lettuce onto the palm of your hand, spoon on a little rice, then a meat roll, and a few of the vegetables. Roll up and dip in sauce. Makes 16 servings.

Bacon Chicken Nuggets

2 boneless, skinless chicken breasts, cut into 24 1-inch cubes
8 slices bacon, cut into thirds
½ cup orange marmalade
¼ cup soy sauce
2 teaspoons sesame oil
1 teaspoon ground ginger
1 garlic clove, minced
Nonstick cooking spray

Wrap each chicken cube with bacon, and secure with a wooden pick. Stir together orange marmalade, soy sauce, sesame oil, ground ginger, and minced garlic in a shallow dish or large freezer bag; add chicken nuggets. Cover or seal, and chill 2 hours, turning occasionally. Coat a rack and broiler pan with cooking spray. Place chicken nuggets on rack. Bake at 450° for 10 minutes; turn and bake 10 more minutes. Makes 24 servings.

Barbecue Chicken Quesadillas

4 (12-inch) flour tortillas
½ cup grated Cheddar cheese, divided
¼ cup grated queso blanco, divided
8 ounces cooked, diced chicken breast
1 red onion, thinly sliced
¼ cup barbecue sauce
Oil for cooking

Lay out 2 of the flour tortillas on a flat surface. Top each with 2 tablespoons Cheddar and the queso blanco, spreading evenly over the tortillas. Divide the chicken among the tortillas, and sprinkle with the desired amount of red onion. Top each with 2 tablespoons barbecue sauce and 2 tablespoons Cheddar. Top with remaining tortillas, and press to seal.

Heat a sauté pan over high heat. Add oil to coat the bottom of the pan, and lower the heat to medium. Cook one quesadilla until golden brown, about 3 minutes per side. Repeat with the other quesadilla. Let cool for 5 minutes. Slice each quesadilla into 4 or 5 pieces. Makes 8 to 10 servings.

Barbecue Chicken Wings

½ cup teriyaki sauce
1 cup oyster sauce
¼ cup soy sauce
¼ cup ketchup
2 tablespoons garlic powder
2 dashes liquid smoke
½ cup sugar
1½ pounds chicken wings, separated at joints, tips discarded
¼ cup honey

In a large bowl, mix the teriyaki sauce, oyster sauce, soy sauce, ketchup, garlic powder, liquid smoke, and sugar. Place the chicken wings in the bowl, cover, and marinate in the refrigerator 8 hours or overnight. Preheat the grill for low heat. Lightly oil the grill grate. Arrange chicken on the grill, and discard the marinade. Grill the chicken wings on one side for 20 minutes; turn and brush with honey. Continue grilling 25 minutes, or until juices run clear. Makes 4 servings.

Blazing Chicken Balls

1 pound ground chicken
½ red bell pepper, finely chopped
1 teaspoon finely chopped chives
½ sweet onion, finely chopped
¼ cup breadcrumbs
1 garlic clove, crushed
1 egg
2 tablespoons hot sauce

Combine all ingredients in a medium-sized mixing bowl. Mix together until well blended. Form into balls and then transfer onto cookie sheet lined with parchment paper. Place on top rack of oven, and bake at 375° for 12 minutes. Makes 12 servings.

Bombay Chicken Pinwheels

1 pound boneless, skinless chicken breasts
1 tablespoon Dijon mustard
1 tablespoon butter, melted
¼ teaspoon salt
⅛ teaspoon black pepper
2 tablespoons butter
¼ cup chutney
½ cup peanut butter
½ cup chicken broth
1 tablespoon honey
¼ teaspoon red pepper flakes
1 garlic clove, crushed

Lightly pound chicken breasts between 2 sheets of waxed paper until about ¼-inch thick. Combine mustard, 1 tablespoon melted butter, salt, and pepper in a small bowl. Spread top side of pounded chicken pieces with mustard mixture. Starting with long edge, tightly roll chicken like a jellyroll. Secure with a small wooden pick. Repeat with remaining chicken.

In a skillet melt 2 tablespoons butter. Add chicken rolls; cook over medium-low heat about 10 minutes, turning, until cooked on all sides. Remove from heat; cool slightly. Cut each roll crosswise into ½-inch thick slices. Insert a small wooden pick into each slice.

In a 1-quart saucepan, combine chutney, peanut butter, broth, honey, red pepper flakes, and garlic. Bring to a boil; simmer 5 minutes. Serve with chicken pinwheels. Makes 8 servings.

Buffalo Chicken Tenders

3 tablespoons Louisiana-style hot pepper sauce
½ teaspoon paprika
¼ teaspoon cayenne pepper
1 pound chicken tenders
½ cup nonfat blue cheese dressing
¼ cup low-fat sour cream
2 tablespoons crumbled blue cheese
1 medium red bell pepper, cut into ½-inch slices

Combine hot pepper sauce, paprika, and cayenne pepper in small bowl; brush on all surfaces of chicken. Place chicken in greased baking dish. Cover; marinate in refrigerator 30 minutes. Bake uncovered at 375° for about 15 minutes, or until chicken is no longer pink in center. Combine dressing, sour cream, and blue cheese in small serving bowl. Garnish as desired. Serve with chicken and bell pepper for dipping. Makes 4 servings.

Cheesy Chicken Biscuit Cups

1 (10-count) can refrigerated biscuits
1 cup cooked, diced chicken breast
1 (10¾-ounce) can cream of chicken soup
⅔ cup low-fat shredded cheddar cheese
½ cup frozen peas, thawed
½ cup chopped onion
⅛ teaspoon black pepper

Separate biscuits and place each in a cup of an ungreased muffin tin, pressing dough up sides to edge of cup. In a medium bowl, combine the rest of the ingredients. Evenly spoon mixture into biscuit cups. Bake at 400° for 12 to 15 minutes until golden brown. Makes 10 servings.

Cherry Tomatoes Stuffed with Apple Chicken Salad

1 pound boneless, skinless chicken breasts
16 cherry tomatoes
2 Granny Smith apples
1 teaspoon lemon juice
Salt and freshly ground black pepper
½ teaspoon ground cinnamon
3 tablespoons mayonnaise
2 teaspoons chopped fresh parsley leaves
16 very small sprigs parsley, for garnish

Poach chicken in water, and set aside to cool. Carefully slice off a small amount of the top of tomatoes, being careful not to remove too much, and scoop out seeds using a ¼-teaspoon measuring spoon. Peel apples, remove core, chop fine, and coat with lemon juice. Finely chop cooled chicken, season with salt, pepper, and cinnamon; stir in mayonnaise and chopped parsley, mixing well. Spoon chicken salad into tomatoes, and garnish with parsley sprigs. Makes 16 servings.

Chicken and Spinach Dip

2 cups cooked, diced chicken breast
1 (8-ounce) package cream cheese, softened
1 cup shredded pepper Jack cheese
1 cup grated Parmesan cheese
6 garlic cloves, pressed
1 (1-ounce) package frozen chopped spinach, thawed and drained
1 large sourdough bun, cut in half and hollowed out

In a medium bowl, combine chicken, cream cheese, pepper Jack cheese, Parmesan cheese, garlic, and spinach. Spoon mixture into bun, packing it tightly; cap with bun top. Wrap bun tightly in foil. Bake at 350° for 20 minutes. Makes 4 to 6 servings.

Chicken and Sweet Potato Croquettes

⅓ cup chopped onion
2 tablespoons unsalted butter
¾ cup all-purpose flour, divided
¼ cup milk
¼ cup chicken broth
2 cups finely chopped cooked chicken or turkey
½ cup mashed sweet potatoes
⅛ teaspoon cayenne pepper
Salt and black pepper
2 large eggs
1 tablespoon water
1½ cups fine fresh breadcrumbs
Vegetable oil for cooking

In a small saucepan, cook the onion in the butter over moderately low heat, stirring, for 5 minutes, stir in ¼ cup of the flour, and cook the roux mixture over low heat, stirring, for 3 minutes. Stir in the milk and the broth, cook the mixture, stirring, until it forms a paste, and cook the paste, stirring, for 3 minutes. Remove the pan from the heat, stir in the chicken, sweet potatoes, cayenne pepper, and salt and black pepper, to taste. Stir to combine.

Cover and chill the chicken mixture for 2 hours, or until it is firm, and roll level tablespoons of it into balls. In a small bowl, beat the eggs and add water. Dredge the balls in the additional ½ cup flour, shaking off the excess, coat them thoroughly with the egg wash, letting the excess drip off, and dredge them in the breadcrumbs, transferring them to wax paper as they are coated.

In a large saucepan heat 2 inches of the oil until a deep-fat thermometer registers 365°. Fry the croquettes in batches for 1 to 1½ minutes, or until they are golden brown, and transfer them with a slotted spoon to paper towels to drain. Makes 8 servings.

Chicken Avocado Egg Rolls

½ cup canola oil
½ cup finely minced red onions
2 tablespoons minced ginger
1 tablespoon minced garlic
¼ cup bamboo shoots
2 cups cooked, diced chicken breast
¼ cup soy sauce
1 cup julienned Napa cabbage
1 cup julienned green cabbage
½ cup bean sprouts
½ cup shredded carrots
¼ cup finely minced red bell peppers
¼ finely chopped celery
4 cups rice bran oil
12 egg roll wrappers
2 avocados, sliced into 24 pieces strips
1 cup egg wash

In a sauté pan over high heat, add oil and red onions. Sauté until translucent. Add ginger, garlic, bamboo shoots, and chicken, and cook for 5 minutes over medium heat. Deglaze pan with soy sauce. Let cool. In medium mixing bowl, combine cabbage, bean sprouts, carrots, peppers, celery, and chicken mixture.

To make egg rolls, lay-out wrapper with corner facing you, and place approximately ¹⁄₁₂th of mixture on roll and then 2 pieces of avocado on top. Fold corner over mixture, and then fold outside corners in, making a roll 4 to 5 inches wide. Roll firmly, being careful not to tear wrapper, and seal the final end with egg wash.

In medium saucepan, heat rice bran oil to 350°. (Oil needs to be deep enough to keep egg roll from touching bottom of pan.) Dredge the egg roll in egg wash, allow excess to drain off, and submerge egg roll in oil. Fry until golden brown, and place on paper towel to drain. Makes 12 servings.

Chicken Corn Mini Pies

3 ounces cream cheese, softened
2 tablespoons mayonnaise
¾ cup cooked, diced chicken
¼ cup chopped onion
½ cup shredded Cheddar cheese
1 (7-ounce) can whole-kernel corn with red and green peppers, drained
1 (8-count) can refrigerated biscuits
Sesame seeds

Lightly grease 8 muffin cups. In medium bowl, blend cream cheese and mayonnaise until smooth. Stir in chicken, onion, cheese, and corn. Separate dough into 8 biscuits. Separate each biscuit into 2 parts by removing the top ⅓ of each biscuit. Place bottom ⅔ piece of each biscuit in greased muffin cup; firmly press in bottom and up the sides, forming ¼-inch rim. Spoon about ⅓ cup chicken mixture into each cup. Top each with remaining ⅓ biscuit, stretching slightly to fit. Press edges to seal. Sprinkle with sesame seeds. Bake at 375° for 15 to 20 minutes until golden brown. Makes 8 servings.

Chicken Crescent Rolls

5 boiled chicken breasts, diced
2 (8-ounce) packages cream cheese, softened
½ cup finely chopped chives
4 tablespoons butter or margarine, softened
5 (8-count) cans crescent rolls

Mix diced chicken, cream cheese, chopped chives, and butter together. Separate rolls in triangles. Place chicken mix on top of each. Roll up as directed on package and pinch ends together. Bake according to package directions. Makes 40 rolls.

Chicken Empanadas

Oil for cooking
6 boneless, skinless chicken thighs, cut into small pieces
2 teaspoons grated fresh ginger
1 garlic clove, minced
⅔ cup chopped green onion
2 teaspoons chopped cilantro
1 teaspoon salt
¼ teaspoon black pepper
2 tomatoes, peeled and chopped
½ cup chopped black olives
½ cup seedless raisins
1 potato, cooked, peeled, and chopped
3 (9-inch) refrigerated pie crusts
1 egg, beaten

In a 10-inch nonstick frying pan, heat oil to medium temperature. Add chicken; sprinkle with ginger, garlic, onion, and cilantro. Cook about 5 minutes without stirring; then stir and cook 5 minutes more. Sprinkle with salt and pepper; add tomatoes and olives. Raise temperature to medium-high, and cook uncovered until liquid is absorbed, about 10 minutes. Stir in potato and raisins; remove from heat and set aside for about 5 minutes to cool slightly.

Cut three 4-inch rounds from each pie shell; make one more circle from scraps from each shell (total 15 rounds). Place ¼ cup of mixture on each round, and fold into half-moon shape (like a turnover). Seal edge by crimping with fork. Brush tops with beaten egg; place on ungreased baking sheet. Bake at 375° about 20 minutes until brown. Serve hot. Makes 15 servings.

Chicken Enchilada Dip

1 pound boneless, skinless chicken breasts
1 (8-ounce) package cream cheese, softened
1 (8-ounce) jar mayonnaise
1 (8-ounce) package shredded Cheddar cheese
1 (4-ounce) can diced green chiles
1 jalapeño, finely diced

Place chicken breasts on a medium baking sheet. Bake at 350° for 20 minutes or until no longer pink. Remove from heat, cool, and shred. Place shredded chicken in a medium bowl, and mix in cream cheese, mayonnaise, Cheddar cheese, green chiles, and jalapeño. Transfer the chicken mixture to a medium baking dish. Bake uncovered in the preheated oven for 30 minutes, or until the edges are golden brown. Makes 4 servings.

Chicken Flautas with Hot Avocado Sauce

4 serrano chiles, stems and seeds removed, chopped
3 teaspoons hot pepper sauce
2 avocados, peeled and coarsely chopped
2 tablespoons chopped onion
½ teaspoon chopped garlic
Vegetable oil for cooking
1 medium onion, chopped
3 garlic cloves, chopped
2 boneless, skinless chicken breasts, poached and shredded
¼ cup chopped fresh cilantro
¼ cup sour cream
1 cup grated Monterey Jack cheese
24 corn tortillas
Vegetable Oil for frying

Combine first 5 ingredients in food processor and purée until smooth. Set aside.

Sauté the onion and garlic in oil until soft, and mix with chicken, cilantro, and sour cream in a bowl. Heat additional oil and fry the tortillas, one at a time, for 5 seconds to soften, being careful they do not become crisp. Overlap two tortillas (cover one half of one with the other), fill with a couple of tablespoons of chicken and a sprinkle of cheese, and roll tightly, securing with toothpicks. Deep fry until crisp and brown, and drain. Remove toothpicks and serve with avocado sauce for dipping. Makes 12 servings.

Chicken Kabobs

¾ cup soy sauce
¼ cup sugar
1 tablespoon vegetable oil
¼ teaspoon garlic powder
½ teaspoon ground ginger
2 boneless, skinless chicken breasts, cut into 1-inch pieces
6 green onions, cut into 1-inch pieces
8 ounces fresh mushrooms, stems removed

In a mixing bowl, combine first 5 ingredients. Stir in chicken and onion; allow to marinate for 30 minutes. On each skewer, thread a piece of chicken, onion, mushroom, and another chicken piece. Place on a broiler rack. Broil 5 inches from the heat, turning and basting with marinade after 3 minutes. Continue broiling for another 3 minutes, or until chicken is done. Serve immediately. Makes 4 servings.

Chicken Lollipops

1 teaspoon salt
1 teaspoon soy sauce
½ teaspoon chili powder
1 drop red food coloring
1 teaspoon distilled white vinegar
1 teaspoon chopped garlic
1 teaspoon finely chopped green chiles
10 chicken wings
4 tablespoons cornstarch

Combine the salt, soy sauce, chili powder, red food coloring, vinegar, garlic, and green chiles. Mix well. Marinate the wings in mixture for at least 30 minutes. Remove the wings, and add the cornstarch to the marinade to make a batter. Dip the wings in the batter, and deep fry. Makes 10 servings.

Chicken Meatballs

2½ cups cooked, minced chicken breast
3 tablespoons finely chopped onion
3 tablespoons finely chopped celery
2 tablespoons finely chopped carrot
2 tablespoons dry breadcrumbs
1 egg white
½ teaspoon poultry seasoning
Dash black pepper

In a bowl, combine all ingredients; mix well. Shape into ¾-inch balls; place on a baking sheet that has been coated with nonstick cooking spray. Bake at 400° for 8 to 10 minutes until lightly browned. Makes 8 servings.

Chicken, Mozzarella, and Pepper Tarts

1 pound ground chicken
¼ cup finely chopped onion
⅓ cup minced red bell pepper
2 tablespoons finely chopped oil-packed sun-dried tomatoes
2 teaspoons dried basil
2 cups finely grated mozzarella cheese
24 prepared tart shells

In a nonstick skillet, cook the chicken just until it turns white. Add the onion, pepper, tomatoes, and basil. Continue to cook until the onions are tender. Remove from heat and let cool. Stir the mozzarella into the cooled chicken mixture, and fill the tart shells. Bake at 350° for 20 to 25 minutes, or until the pastry is golden brown and the filling is bubbly. Makes 24 servings.

Chicken Pups

8 chicken breast tenders
1 tablespoon prepared mustard
1 (11½-ounce) tube refrigerated cornbread twist dough
2 tablespoons ketchup

Line baking sheet with aluminum foil, and coat with nonstick cooking spray. Toss chicken in mustard. Lay on baking sheet. Bake at 400° for 8 minutes. Cool.

Unroll cornbread dough. Pinch center seam together to form 8 long strips of dough. Spread ketchup on 1 side of each strip. Wrap dough around each chicken tender, ketchup side to chicken. Pinch ends of dough to seal. Bake 11 to 13 minutes, until chicken is done and dough browns. Makes 8 servings.

Chicken Sandwich Ring

1 cup mayonnaise
2 tablespoons Dijon mustard
2 tablespoons chopped fresh parsley
1½ tablespoons finely chopped green onions
1 cup cooked, diced chicken breast
6 slices bacon, cooked crispy, crumbled
1 cup shredded Monterey Jack cheese, divided
2 (8-ounce) packages crescent roll dough
2 medium Roma tomatoes
1 medium red or yellow bell pepper, as bowl
2 cups shredded lettuce

In a medium bowl, mix mayonnaise, mustard, parsley, and onion. Set aside. In a large bowl, mix chicken, bacon, ¾ cup of cheese, and ⅓ cup of mayonnaise mixture. Mix well and set aside.

Open and unroll crescent roll dough, and separate into triangles. Arrange triangles in a circle on a round baking stone (or a greased pizza pan if you do not have a baking stone) with the wide ends of triangles overlapping in the center and points hanging over outside edge, leaving at least a 5- to 6-inch clear circle in the center of the stone. Spoon chicken mixture evenly onto dough, onto the wide ends of the triangles.

Wrap pointed ends of dough around chicken mixture, and tuck under the wide ends of the dough, forming a closed ring with slits around the outside edge, where filling shows through in places. Slice Roma tomatoes into enough wedges to place one wedge in each open slit around the ring.

Bake at 375° for 20 to 25 minutes until golden brown. Remove from oven, and sprinkle with remaining cheese. Set aside. Remove top from bell pepper, and clean out seeds. Wash and dry pepper with a paper towel. Fill pepper with mayonnaise mixture, and place in center of sandwich ring; fill in the space between the pepper and the sandwich ring with the shredded lettuce. Serve in wedges with the mayonnaise dip. Makes 12 servings.

Chicken Squares

1 (3-ounce) cream cheese, softened
2 tablespoons butter, softened
Salt and black pepper, to taste
2 cups cooked, diced chicken breast
¾ cup crushed croutons
2 tablespoons milk
1 tablespoon chopped onions
¼ cup chopped olives (optional)
1 (12-count) can refrigerated crescent dinner rolls
1 tablespoon butter, melted

Blend cream cheese with 2 tablespoons butter until smooth. Add salt and pepper, chicken, croutons, milk, onion, and olives, and mix well. Spoon ½ cup meat mixture onto 2 unseparated triangles of dough. Pull 4 corners to the top, twist slightly, and seal edges by pinching. Brush tops with the melted butter. Bake on ungreased cookie sheet at 350° for 20 to 25 minutes. Makes 6 servings.

Chicken Wings

5 pounds chicken wings, each wing cut into 3 pieces
2 cups brown sugar
½ cup mustard
½ cup ketchup
¼ cup Worcestershire sauce

Put chicken in a slow cooker. Combine remaining ingredients, and pour over chicken. Cook on low for 6 to 8 hours. Makes 10 servings.

Chinese Chicken in Foil

1½ pounds boneless, skinless chicken breasts
2 green onions, finely chopped
40 to 50 small pieces aluminum foil (5 x 5 inches)
1 tablespoon hoisin sauce
1 tablespoon soy sauce
1 tablespoon orange juice
1 tablespoon oil
1 teaspoon sesame oil
1 garlic clove, minced
¼ teaspoon black pepper
1 teaspoon sugar
2 teaspoons cornstarch

Cut chicken into 1-inch cubes. Place in a shallow pan. Sprinkle green onions on top. Mix remaining ingredients and pour over chicken. Marinate for 2 hours at room temperature or overnight in the refrigerator. Wrap each piece of chicken in a piece of foil. Place in a single layer on a cookie sheet. Bake at 450° for 12 minutes. Makes 6 servings.

Cilantro Chicken Kabobs

2½ pounds boneless, skinless chicken breasts
1 teaspoon salt
1 lemon
6 tablespoons plain yogurt
1 (1-inch) piece fresh ginger, peeled and grated
3 garlic cloves, crushed
1 teaspoon ground cumin
½ teaspoon cayenne pepper
½ teaspoon garam masala
1 tablespoon besan
4 green chiles, stemmed and sliced
1 cup cilantro, stems removed
½ cup unsalted butter, melted
Sliced onion and cucumber, for garnish

Cut each breast in half lengthwise and then cut each half crosswise into three or four equal pieces. Lay the pieces in a single layer on a platter. Sprinkle the salt and the juice from the lemon over them, and rub into the chicken. Set aside for 20 minutes. Meanwhile, put the yogurt in a small bowl. Beat it with a fork or whisk until it is smooth and creamy. Add the ginger, garlic, cumin, cayenne, garam masala, and besan. Stir.

Make a paste out of the green chiles, cilantro, and ¼ cup of water in a food processor. Add the paste to the yogurt mixture. After the chicken has rested for 20 minutes, hold a sieve over the chicken pieces and pour the yogurt mixture into the sieve and push through as much as you can with a rubber spatula. Mix well with the chicken pieces, and refrigerate for 6 to 24 hours in an airtight container.

Thread the chicken pieces on skewers. Brush the chicken with half the melted butter, and broil for about 7 minutes. Turn the chicken pieces over, brush with the rest of the butter, and broil for another 8 to 10 minutes. Serve with thick slices of onions and cucumbers. Makes 4 to 6 servings.

Coconut Chicken Balls

1 pound boneless, skinless chicken breasts
1 tablespoon cornstarch
1 teaspoon ground coriander
½ teaspoon salt
¼ cup all-purpose flour
2 egg whites
2 tablespoon honey
1½ cups sweetened shredded coconut
1 (12-ounce jar) orange marmalade

Cut up each chicken breast into 8 pieces. Cover a cookie sheet with aluminum foil, and spray with vegetable cooking spray. In a plastic bag, mix together cornstarch, coriander, salt, and flour. In a bowl, mix the egg whites and honey. Place the coconut in a second bowl. Place chicken pieces in bag and shake. Coat pieces in the egg and honey mixture. Roll chicken in coconut and place on a cookie sheet. Cook at 400° for 17 minutes or until thermometer reads 170°. Cool slightly, and lightly coat with orange marmalade. Spear with long toothpicks. Makes 16 servings.

Creamy Chicken and Jalapeño Nachos

12 ounces cream cheese, softened
2 jalapeños, seeded and minced
3 tablespoons chopped red onion
2 garlic cloves, minced
1 teaspoon ground cumin
1 teaspoon chili powder
1½ cups grated Monterey Jack cheese
1 pound cooked, diced chicken breasts
Salt and black pepper, to taste
6 small pita breads, cut and separated into two rounds each

Combine the cream cheese, jalapeños, onion, garlic, cumin, chili powder, and cheese in a large mixing bowl. Beat with an electric mixer on a low speed until blended. Stir in diced chicken. Season with salt and pepper. Spread each pita round with a generous amount of the filling. Bake on cookie sheets at 375° until puffed and bubbling, about 8 minutes. Immediately cut into wedges and serve. Makes 12 servings.

Creamy Chicken Mini Pitas

2 pounds roasted chicken meat, chopped
½ cup finely chopped celery
2 scallions, finely chopped
½ cup finely chopped walnuts
1 tablespoon finely chopped tarragon leaves
⅔ cup mayonnaise
Salt and black pepper, to taste
15 mini pita breads

In a medium bowl, combine the chicken, celery, scallions, walnuts, tarragon, and mayonnaise; mix thoroughly. If the mixture is not creamy enough, add more mayonnaise. Season with salt and pepper, cover, and refrigerate for 1 hour. Slice the mini pitas in half, open the pockets, and stuff with a heaping tablespoon of chicken mixture. Makes 15 servings.

Crunchy Parmesan Chicken Tenders

4 tablespoons plus ½ cup extra-virgin olive oil, divided
1 cup buttermilk
1½ pounds chicken tenders
3 large garlic cloves, minced
½ teaspoon salt
3 tablespoons balsamic vinegar
Black pepper, to taste
1¼ cups freshly grated Parmesan
¾ cup Italian-style breadcrumbs

Brush 1 tablespoon of oil over each of 2 heavy baking sheets lined with foil. Place the buttermilk in a large bowl. Add the chicken tenders, and stir to coat. Let stand at least 15 minutes and up to 30 minutes.

Meanwhile, mash the garlic with the salt in a medium bowl. Whisk in the vinegar and then the remaining ½ cup of oil. Season the vinaigrette with pepper, and transfer vinaigrette to a small serving bowl. Stir the Parmesan and breadcrumbs in a pie dish. Remove the chicken tenders from the buttermilk and dredge them in the breadcrumb mixture to coat completely. Arrange the coated chicken tenders on the prepared baking sheets, spacing evenly. Drizzle the remaining 2 tablespoons of oil over the chicken tenders, and bake at 400° until golden brown, about 12 minutes. Transfer the chicken tenders to a platter, and serve the vinaigrette alongside for dipping. Makes 4 to 6 servings.

Curried Manapua Puffs

1 (10-ounce) can chunk chicken, drained and flaked
½ cup finely chopped green onions
1 (8-ounce) can sliced water chestnuts, drained and finely chopped
2 tablespoons oyster sauce
2 tablespoons toasted sesame seeds
1½ teaspoons curry powder
Salt and black pepper, to taste
5 (10-count) packages refrigerated biscuit dough

In a medium bowl, mix together chicken, green onions, water chestnuts, oyster sauce, sesame seeds, curry powder, salt, and pepper.
Lightly grease a large baking sheet. Flatten each biscuit, place approximately 1 teaspoon of the chicken mixture onto each biscuit, and pinch the dough around the mixture to form an encasing ball. Place on baking sheet, leaving about 2 inches between each biscuit, and bake at 400° for 10 to 15 minutes, or until golden brown. Makes 50 mini puffs.

Easy BBQ Wings

2 pounds small chicken legs
Barbecue sauce
Ranch salad dressing

Arrange the chicken legs on the rack of a roasting pan. Using a brush, coat both sides of each chicken leg with the barbecue sauce. Bake at 325° for 30 minutes until tender. Serve with dressing for dipping. Makes about 6 servings.

Easy Chicken Cheese Ball

2 (8-ounce) packages cream cheese, softened
1 (1-ounce) package ranch dressing mix
1 (5-ounce) can chunk chicken, drained
½ cup chopped pecans

In a medium bowl, combine cream cheese, dressing mix, and chicken. Form the mixture into a ball. On a cutting board or a piece of wax paper, spread the chopped pecans. Roll the ball in the pecans until fully coated. Wrap the ball in plastic, and chill for at least 1 hour. Makes 3 cups.

Enchilada Dip

2 pounds boneless, skinless chicken thighs
1 (10-ounce) can enchilada sauce
2 (8-ounce) packages cream cheese, softened
4 cups shredded pepper Jack cheese

Combine chicken and enchilada sauce in a slow cooker. Cover and cook on low for 8 to 10 hours, or until chicken is thoroughly cooked. Using two forks, shred chicken in the sauce. Cut cream cheese into cubes and stir into the slow cooker, along with the Cheddar cheese; mix well. Cover and cook on low for 30 minutes, stirring twice, until mixture is blended and cheese is melted. Makes 12 servings.

Ginger Chicken Pot Stickers

3 cups finely shredded cabbage
1 egg white, lightly beaten
1 tablespoon citrus-seasoned soy sauce or light soy sauce
¼ teaspoon red pepper flakes
1 tablespoon minced fresh ginger
4 green onions with tops, finely chopped
¼ pound ground chicken, cooked and drained
24 wonton wrappers, at room temperature
Cornstarch
½ cup water
1 tablespoon oyster sauce
½ teaspoon honey
⅛ teaspoon red pepper flakes
2 teaspoons grated lemon peel
1 tablespoon peanut oil

Steam cabbage 5 minutes, and cool to room temperature. Squeeze out any excess moisture; set aside. To prepare filling, combine egg white, soy sauce, ¼ teaspoon red pepper, ginger, and green onions in large bowl; blend well. Stir in cabbage and chicken.

To prepare pot stickers, place 1 tablespoon filling in center of 1 wonton wrapper. Gather edges around filling, pressing firmly at top to seal. Repeat with remaining wrappers and filling. Place pot stickers on large baking sheet dusted with cornstarch. Refrigerate 1 hour until cold. Meanwhile, to prepare sauce, combine remaining ingredients except oil in small bowl; mix well. Set aside.

Heat oil in large nonstick skillet over high heat. Add pot stickers and cook until bottoms are golden brown. Pour sauce over top. Cover and cook 3 minutes. Uncover and cook until all liquid is absorbed. Makes 24 servings.

Green Chile Pepper and Tomato Chicken Dip

1 (2-pound) package processed cheese, cubed
1 (15-ounce) can turkey chili
2 (10-ounce) cans tomatoes with diced green chiles
2 (10-ounce) cans chunk chicken, drained and flaked
1 cup sour cream

In a double boiler, melt the processed cheese. Blend in the turkey chili and diced tomatoes with green chiles. Mix in chicken and sour cream. Heat and stir until well blended. Serve warm. Makes 6 cups.

Island Chicken Appetizers

1 (10-ounce) jar apricot preserves
1 (8-ounce) bottle Thousand Island salad dressing
1 (1-ounce) package onion soup mix
8 boneless, skinless chicken breasts

Mix preserves, dressing, and soup mix in saucepan. Cook over medium heat 10 minutes, stirring occasionally. Place chicken in a greased baking dish, and pour dressing over top, thoroughly coating chicken. Bake at 350° for 15 to 20 minutes. Makes 8 servings.

Mini Chicken Pot Pies

⅓ cup chicken broth
1 cup frozen mixed vegetables (corn, peas, carrots)
2 (10-ounce) cans chicken breast, drained
½ (10¾-ounce) can cream of celery soup
1 tablespoon garlic herb seasoning blend
¼ cup butter, melted
5 sheets phyllo dough
Pepper

In a medium saucepan, heat the chicken broth. Add frozen vegetables and chicken, and simmer for 15 minutes on medium heat. Add soup and herb seasoning blend, and cook for another 5 minutes. Set aside.

Arrange 12 ovenproof espresso or demitasse cups on a sheet pan lined with parchment paper. Leave about 2 inches of space between cups. Fill each cup with 1 heaping tablespoon chicken vegetable mixture. Gently brush melted butter over each sheet of phyllo dough and cut each into 3-inch squares. Top each cup with 5 phyllo squares, and fold ends toward sides of cup. Bake chicken pot pies at 375° for 25 minutes or until phyllo turns golden brown and sheets puff up. Serve warm. Makes 12 servings.

Party Tray Pita Pockets with Smoked Chicken

8 ounce boneless, skinless chicken breast
1 tablespoon butter
Salt and black pepper, to taste
Liquid smoke
1 celery stalk, finely chopped
4 tablespoons thinly sliced green onion
⅓ cup finely chopped red bell pepper
4 tablespoons mayonnaise
Zest of 1 lemon
3 teaspoons fresh lemon juice
⅛ teaspoon freshly ground black pepper
Salt, to taste
1 (6-count) packet pita pockets
3 cups shredded arugula or romaine lettuce
2 tablespoons almonds, chopped and toasted
Lettuce leaves for garnish

In a small skillet over medium-high heat, sauté chicken in butter until done; add salt, pepper and drizzle with liquid smoke; dice fine; add to a small bowl with celery, green onion, and red bell pepper. Stir in mayonnaise, lemon zest, lemon juice, pepper, and salt.

Cut pita pockets in half; cut thin strips from the bottom to sit square on a plate. Fill pockets with shredded arugula and chicken mixture, top with almonds, and serve on a bed of lettuce leaves. Makes 12 servings.

Pecan Chicken Tenders

½ cup butter
1 cup all-purpose flour
1 teaspoon baking powder
2 teaspoons garlic salt
2 teaspoons paprika
½ teaspoon black pepper
½ cup chopped pecans
1 tablespoon toasted sesame seeds
1 egg, beaten
½ cup milk
6 boneless, skinless chicken breasts, cut into strips

Melt butter in a large glass baking dish at 375°; set aside. Combine flour, baking powder, garlic salt, paprika, pepper, pecans, and sesame seeds in a large shallow dish. Combine egg and milk in a separate dish. Dip each chicken breast strip in egg mixture, and then dredge in flour mixture. Place in prepared baking dish. Bake about 25 minutes until cooked through. Makes 12 servings.

Pepperoni Chicken Rollups

4 boneless, skinless chicken breasts, pounded thin
Dash garlic powder
Salt and black pepper, to taste
1 teaspoon Italian seasoning
20 slices pepperoni
1 cup chopped pepperoni
4 slices mozzarella cheese
1 (28-ounce) jar spaghetti sauce

Season chicken with garlic powder, salt, pepper, and Italian seasoning. Place 4 to 5 slices pepperoni on each breast and top with a slice of cheese. Roll up breasts and fasten with toothpicks.

Fry the chopped pepperoni in a medium skillet, until it has released most of its oil. Remove pepperoni from skillet, and set aside. Brown chicken rolls in pepperoni oil about 5 to 10 minutes each side. Place chicken in a baking dish. Combine spaghetti sauce and chopped pepperoni, and pour over chicken. Bake at 350° for 30 to 40 minutes. Makes 4 servings.

Pico de Gallo Chicken Quesadillas

2 tomatoes, diced
1 onion, finely chopped
2 limes, juiced
2 tablespoons chopped fresh cilantro
1 jalapeño, seeded and minced
Salt and black pepper, to taste
2 tablespoons olive oil, divided
2 boneless, skinless chicken breasts, cut into strips
½ onion, thinly sliced
1 green bell pepper, thinly sliced
2 garlic cloves, minced
4 (12-inch) flour tortillas
1 cup shredded Monterey Jack cheese
¼ cup sour cream, for topping

In a small bowl, combine tomatoes, onion, lime juice, cilantro, jalapeño, salt, and pepper. Set aside. In a large skillet, heat 1 tablespoon olive oil. Add chicken and sauté, until cooked through and juices run clear. Remove chicken from skillet and set aside.

Put the remaining 1 tablespoon olive oil in the hot skillet, and sauté the sliced onion and green pepper until tender. Stir in the minced garlic, and sauté until the aroma is strong. Mix in half of the pico de gallo and chicken breast meat. Set aside; keep warm.

In a heavy skillet, heat one flour tortilla. Spread ¼ cup shredded cheese on the tortilla, and top with ½ the chicken mixture. Sprinkle another ¼ cup cheese over the chicken, and top with another tortilla. When bottom tortilla is lightly brown and cheese has started to melt, flip quesadilla and cook on the opposite side. Remove quesadilla from skillet, and cut into quarters.

Repeat with remaining quesadillas. Serve quesadillas with sour cream and remaining pico de gallo. Makes 16 servings.

Pineapple Chicken Bites

1 pound boneless, skinless chicken breasts, cut into cubes
1 to 2 tablespoons vegetable oil
2 (8-ounce) packages refrigerated crescent roll dough
1 (8-ounce) can pineapple chunks, drained, with juice reserved
3 tablespoons honey
1 tablespoon ground ginger

Place chicken in a large, deep skillet with vegetable oil. Cook over medium-high heat until no longer pink. Drain and set aside.

Separate crescent roll dough into individual triangles. Place triangles in a single layer on a large baking sheet. In a small bowl, mix 3 teaspoons reserved pineapple juice, honey, and ginger. Brush each triangle with the pineapple juice mixture. Place one pineapple chunk and approximately 1 tablespoon chicken meat on each triangle. Roll and seal each triangle individually. Bake at 350° for 15 minutes until golden brown. Makes 12 servings.

Polynesian Pineapple Chicken Bacon Skewers

¼ cup soy sauce
2 tablespoons honey
Juice of half a lime
1 teaspoon red pepper flakes
½ teaspoon ground ginger
1 pineapple, sliced into chunks
1 pound bacon, cut into pieces
2 boneless, skinless chicken breasts, cut into cubes
1 package cherry tomatoes

Combine soy sauce, honey, lime juice, red pepper flakes, and ginger. Wrap each pineapple chunk in bacon. Assemble each skewer as follows: pineapple chunk wrapped in bacon, chicken cube, and cherry tomato. Repeat until skewer is full. Place skewers on a broiler pan. Broil for 5 to 7 minutes, turn skewers, and drizzle with soy glaze. Place back under the broiler for an additional 5 to 7 minutes, until bacon is crispy and chicken is cooked through. Remove and set aside. Makes 16 servings.

Pretzel Chicken Chunks

4 boneless, skinless chicken breasts
¾ cup prepared Dijon mustard
2 tablespoons honey
¼ teaspoon cayenne pepper
¼ teaspoon garlic salt
¾ cup crushed pretzels

Cut the chicken into 1-inch cubes. Line a baking sheet with aluminum foil. In a small bowl, combine mustard, honey, cayenne pepper, and garlic salt. Mix together, and set half of mixture aside to be used as dipping sauce.

Coat chicken chunks completely in remaining mustard mixture, and roll in pretzel crumbs. Place coated chicken on prepared baking sheet. Bake at 350° for 10 minutes until golden brown. Serve with reserved mustard dip. Makes 16 servings.

Raspberry Chicken Salsa Torte

1 tablespoon olive oil
1 onion, cut into strips
2 garlic cloves, minced
3 cups grated zucchini
¾ pound boneless, skinless chicken breasts, cooked and shredded
3 cups shredded Monterey Jack cheese
3 (10-inch) flour tortillas
1 (16-ounce) jar raspberry salsa
Sour cream (optional)

In a large skillet, heat oil, and sauté onion and garlic for 5 minutes. Add zucchini and sauté for another 5 minutes, stirring occasionally. Drain well and stir in chicken; set aside.

Spray a 10-inch pie plate with cooking spray. Spread half of the chicken mixture into it, then sprinkle with half of the cheese. Place 1 tortilla on top of the cheese layer, spread on half of the salsa, and add 1 more tortilla. Spread the remaining salsa and the remaining chicken mixture over the tortilla. Top with 1 more tortilla and sprinkle with the remaining cheese.

Cover with foil and bake at 400° for 40 minutes. Remove foil and bake for an additional 15 minutes. Let cool for 10 minutes. Cut into wedges and serve with sour cream. Makes 8 servings.

Ritzy Chicken Livers

12 fresh chicken livers
24 buttery round crackers, crushed
1 tablespoon Italian seasoning
4 tablespoons butter, melted

Place crushed cracker crumbs and seasoning in a shallow bowl or plate. Pour melted butter into another shallow bowl or plate. Roll chicken livers in butter or margarine and then in crumbs. Place coated chicken in a lightly greased baking dish. Bake at 350° for 40 to 45 minutes. Makes 12 servings.

Saucy Chicken Dip

1 tablespoon vegetable oil
3 boneless, skinless chicken breasts, cut into cubes
1 cup shredded mozzarella cheese
1 cup shredded Cheddar cheese
1 (10¾-ounce) can condensed cream of chicken soup
1 banana pepper, chopped

Heat the oil in a medium skillet over medium-high heat. Cook the cubed chicken until no longer pink, 5 to 10 minutes. Drain chicken and place it in a medium baking dish with mozzarella cheese, Cheddar cheese, soup, and banana pepper. Bake uncovered at 350° for 20 to 25 minutes until bubbly and lightly browned. Makes 12 servings.

Savory Italian Wings

1½ cups cracker crumbs
1 cup grated Parmesan cheese
1 (1-ounce) envelope Italian dressing mix
2 pounds chicken wings
½ cup butter, melted

Combine crumbs, cheese, and Italian dressing mix. Coat wings with melted butter and then crumb mixture. Bake on greased baking sheet at 350° for about 30 minutes. Makes about 6 servings.

Savory Ranch Wings

1½ cups cracker crumbs
1 cup grated Parmesan cheese
1 (1-ounce) envelope ranch dressing mix
2 pounds chicken wings
½ cup butter, melted

Combine crumbs, cheese, and ranch dressing mix. Coat wings with melted butter and then crumb mixture. Bake on greased baking sheet at 350° for about 30 minutes. Makes about 6 servings.

Savory Southwestern Wings

1½ cups cracker crumbs
1 cup grated Parmesan cheese
2 teaspoons chili powder
2 teaspoons ground cumin
2 teaspoons garlic salt
2 pounds chicken wings
½ cup butter, melted

Combine crumbs, cheese, chili powder, cumin, and garlic salt. Coat wings with melted butter and then crumb mixture. Bake on greased baking sheet at 350° for about 30 minutes. Makes about 6 servings.

Smoky Rollups

12 slices smoked beef
6 boneless, skinless chicken breasts, pounded thin and cut in half
  lengthwise
½ cup ketchup
½ cup mayonnaise
½ cup apricot jam

Trim the fat from the smoked meat; place a slice on each chicken piece.
Starting at narrow end, roll up each piece. Fasten with toothpicks and place
seam-side down in a large baking dish. Mix ketchup, mayonnaise, and jam
together. Pour mixture over chicken and bake uncovered at 350° for 20 to 25
minutes. Makes 12 servings.

Spanikopita Chicken Meatballs with Spicy Yogurt Sauce

1 small onion, finely chopped
4 garlic cloves, chopped and divided
¾ cup crumbled feta cheese
1 pound ground chicken
1 tablespoon poultry seasoning
1 tablespoon extra-virgin olive oil, plus some for drizzling
1 (10-ounce) box frozen chopped spinach, thawed and drained
1½ cups Greek-style plain yogurt
⅓ seedless cucumber, peeled and chopped
3 tablespoons fresh dill
½ lemon, juiced
1½ teaspoons ground cumin
1½ teaspoons ground coriander
Salt, to taste

In a large bowl, combine onion and 3 cloves of garlic. Add feta, chicken, poultry seasoning, and a liberal drizzle of extra-virgin olive oil. Mix the meat with the spinach and feta, and form 18 (1½-inch) meatballs. Place the meatballs on a nonstick baking sheet, and bake at 400° for 10 to 12 minutes, until they are golden and juices run clear.

Meanwhile, combine yogurt, remaining garlic, cucumber, dill, lemon juice, cumin, coriander, and salt in food processor, and process until smooth. Adjust seasonings. Serve meatballs alongside sauce with toothpicks. Makes 18 servings.

Spicy Chicken and Cilantro Wontons

2 pounds boneless, skinless chicken thighs, diced
3 stalks lemongrass, cut into 1-inch pieces
¼ cup chopped fresh ginger
6 garlic cloves, peeled
1 fresh red chile pepper, chopped
1 cup fresh chopped cilantro
¼ cup soy sauce
1 tablespoon sesame oil
50 wonton wrappers
1 quart vegetable oil, for frying

In a food processor, combine the chicken, lemongrass, ginger, garlic, chile pepper, cilantro, soy sauce, and sesame oil. Pulse until thoroughly mixed and chicken is minced.

Separate all of the wonton wrappers, and lay them out on a clean surface. Set a bowl of water to the side to dip your fingers. Place about 1 teaspoon of the chicken mixture onto the center of each wrapper. Wet the edges by dipping your fingers in water and wiping the edge of each wrapper. Fold over into triangles, and press to seal. Take the two opposing points of the triangle, and fold around to join together.

Heat the oil in a deep-frying pot. Fry several wontons at a time, turning as needed, until lightly browned. Remove to drain on paper towels. Serve while hot. Makes 50 servings.

Spicy Chicken and Cheese Balls

1 tablespoon vegetable oil
1 small onion, chopped
1 pound ground chicken
3 cups biscuit mix
1½ cups shredded Colby or Monterey Jack cheese
1 teaspoon minced garlic
½ teaspoon red pepper flakes

Heat oil in a skillet over medium heat. Sauté onion until soft and translucent; transfer to a large bowl. Add ground chicken, biscuit mix, shredded cheese, garlic, and red pepper flakes. Mix well and form into 1-inch balls. Place on a nonstick baking pan. Bake at 350° for 15 to 20 minutes until browned. Makes 6 servings.

Spicy Chicken Wings

2 cups brown sugar
¼ cup hot pepper sauce
½ cup butter
4 tablespoons soy sauce
4 pounds chicken wings

In a saucepan, combine the brown sugar, hot sauce, butter, and soy sauce. Heat until butter is melted. Place the chicken wings in a slow cooker, and pour sauce over top. Cover and cook on low for 4 to 5 hours. Makes 12 servings.

Strawberry Pineapple Chicken Bites

2 tablespoons olive oil
2 pounds boneless, skinless chicken breasts, cut into small chunks
1 (12-ounce) jar strawberry preserves
1 (8-ounce) jar chile sauce
1 (8-ounce) can pineapple chunks
Salt and black pepper, to taste

Heat the olive oil in a skillet over medium-high heat. Cook the chicken in oil for 5 minutes until browned on all sides. Reduce heat to medium, and pour in the preserves and chile sauce. Cook, stirring occasionally, for 10 minutes. Add the pineapple chunks to the skillet. Season with salt and pepper. Continue cooking 2 minutes, until heated through. Serve with toothpicks. Makes 12 servings.

Sweet and Gooey Chicken Wings

½ cup soy sauce
¼ cup packed brown sugar
½ tablespoon vegetable oil
½ teaspoon minced fresh ginger
½ teaspoon garlic powder
1½ pounds chicken wings

In a casserole, combine soy sauce, brown sugar, oil, ginger, and garlic powder. Mix until brown sugar completely dissolves. Place the chicken wings in the dish, and turn them over until they are all well coated. Cover and refrigerate for at least 4 hours, turning after 2 hours. Bake covered at 350° for 45 minutes. Turn the chicken wings, and spoon sauce from the bottom of the pan over the tops of the wings. Cook uncovered an additional 50 minutes. Makes 4 servings.

Thai Chicken Spring Rolls

1 cup peanut sauce
1 (1½-inch) piece fresh ginger, peeled and minced
2 garlic cloves, minced
1 teaspoon soy sauce
1 pound boneless, skinless chicken breasts, cut into 1-inch pieces
1 teaspoon peanut oil
6 ounces fresh snow peas
12 ounces bean sprouts
4 green onion, chopped
1 pound watercress, chopped
¼ cup chopped fresh cilantro
2 large carrots
1 teaspoon soy sauce
1 teaspoon peanut oil
12 spring roll wrappers
½ cup peanut sauce

Combine 1 cup peanut sauce, ginger, garlic, and 1 teaspoon soy sauce in a large bowl. Add chicken and mix until coated. Place in refrigerator to marinate for 30 minutes. Heat 1 teaspoon peanut oil in a wok or skillet over medium heat. Cook the snow peas, bean sprouts, and green onion until heated but still crisp, 3 to 4 minutes. Transfer to another large bowl. Mix in the watercress and cilantro. Use a vegetable peeler to cut long strips of carrot and add to bowl. Drizzle 1 teaspoon soy sauce into the watercress mixture; toss to coat. Heat 1 teaspoon of oil to the wok or skillet. Cook the marinated chicken until no longer pink inside, about 10 minutes. Fill a large bowl with hot water. Dip wrappers one at a time into the water for about 2 seconds each. As wrappers are removed from the water, fill each with 2 large spoonfuls of the chicken and a small handful of the watercress mixture. Fold in two opposite ends of the wrapper to meet the filling. Then fold the bottom of the wrapper over the top of the filling and roll. Serve with peanut sauce for dipping. Makes 12 servings.

Tiny Chicken Turnovers

3 tablespoons chopped onion
3 tablespoons butter
1¾ cups cooked, shredded chicken breast
3 tablespoons chicken broth
¼ teaspoon garlic salt
¼ teaspoon poultry seasoning
¼ teaspoon black pepper
1 (3-ounce) package cream cheese, softened
1½ cups all-purpose flour
½ teaspoon salt
½ teaspoon paprika
1 cup butter, chilled
5 tablespoons cold water

In a large skillet, sauté the onion in the butter until tender. Stir in the chicken, chicken broth, garlic salt, poultry seasoning, pepper, and cream cheese. Remove from heat and set aside.

In a large bowl, mix together the flour, salt, and paprika; cut in butter until mixture resembles coarse crumbs. Gradually add water, tossing with a fork until a ball forms. On a floured surface, roll out the pastry to ¹⁄₁₆-inch thickness. Cut with a 2½-inch round cookie or biscuit cutter. Reroll scraps and cut more circles until the pastry is used up. Mound a heaping teaspoon of filling on half of each circle. Moisten edges with water and fold pastry over filling to make a half-moon shape. Press edges with a fork to seal. Prick tops with a fork for steam vents.

Place turnovers on a baking sheet and bake at 375° for 15 to 20 minutes until golden brown. Makes 2½ dozen.

Yakitori

2 tablespoons soy sauce
1½ tablespoons sugar
2 tablespoons water
2 boneless, skinless chicken breasts, cut into 1-inch pieces
Bamboo skewers, soaked in water

Combine soy sauce, sugar, and water; pour over chicken pieces; marinate 2 hours or more. Thread chicken onto skewers, and broil or grill 7 to 8 minutes, turning once. Makes 6 servings.

SALADS

Apple Chicken Salad

5 to 6 ounces cooked, cubed chicken
¼ cup chopped apple
½ cup thinly sliced celery
2 tablespoons raisins
⅓ cup Italian dressing
2 teaspoons brown sugar
Lettuce leaves
Pecans or almonds, chopped

In a medium bowl, gently stir together chicken, apple, celery, and raisins. In a small bowl, whisk together dressing and brown sugar; pour over chicken mixture. Toss gently to coat. Serve on lettuce leaves. Top with chopped nuts. Makes 2 servings.

Asian Chicken Salad

2½ cups cooked chicken in bite-size pieces
1 (10-ounce) bag shredded cabbage
1 cup sliced mushrooms
2 carrots, shredded
2 tablespoons chopped cilantro
1 cucumber, thinly sliced
½ cup nonfat Oriental-style salad dressing
Black pepper to taste
3 green onions, thinly sliced
1 tangerine, peeled and sectioned

In a large bowl combine chicken, cabbage, mushrooms, carrot, cilantro, cucumber, dressing, and black pepper. Toss well. Top with green onions and tangerine sections. Makes 4 servings.

Chicken and Fruit Salad

½ cup plain nonfat yogurt
½ to 1 teaspoon lemon pepper seasoning
½ teaspoon dry mustard
¼ teaspoon garlic salt
¼ teaspoon poppy seed
1¼ teaspoons artificial sweetener
1 to 2 tablespoons orange juice
4 cups torn spinach leaves
1 cup thinly sliced cooked chicken breast
2 cups sliced strawberries
1 cup halved seedless green grapes
1½ cups thinly sliced yellow summer squash
2 medium oranges, peeled and sectioned
½ cup toasted pecan pieces (optional)

Combine yogurt, lemon pepper seasoning, mustard, garlic salt, poppy seed, and artificial sweetener in a small bowl. Add enough orange juice to reach drizzling consistency; set aside. Line platter with spinach. Arrange chicken, strawberries, grapes, squash, and orange sections over spinach. Drizzle salad with dressing. Sprinkle with pecans, if desired. Makes 4 servings.

Chicken and Melon–Stuffed Shells

1 medium cantaloupe
8 dried jumbo pasta shells
1 cup cooked, cubed chicken
½ cup peeled and finely chopped honeydew melon
¼ cup plain low-fat yogurt
2 tablespoons fresh lemon juice
1 tablespoon snipped fresh chives
1 teaspoon Dijon mustard
Fresh thyme sprigs (optional)

Cut each cantaloupe half into thirds. Cover and chill 4 of the wedges until ready to serve. Peel and chop the remaining 2 wedges; set aside. Cook pasta shells according to package directions; drain. Rinse with cold water; drain again. Meanwhile, in a large bowl, combine chopped cantaloupe, chicken, honeydew melon, yogurt, lemon juice, chives, and mustard. Spoon about ¼ cup of the chicken mixture into each cooked pasta shell. To serve, arrange 2 filled pasta shells and a cantaloupe wedge on each dinner plate. If desired, garnish with fresh thyme. Makes 4 servings.

Chicken, Black Bean, and Corn Salad

1 (15½-ounce) can black beans, drained and rinsed
1 cup cooked corn
2 pounds chicken breasts, grilled and cubed
¼ cup minced cilantro sprigs
¼ cup minced bottled roasted red pepper or pimento
½ cup plain yogurt
½ cup mayonnaise
1 teaspoon minced canned chipotle in adobo sauce
1 teaspoon adobo sauce
3 avocados, halved and pitted

In a large bowl, toss together black beans, corn, chicken, cilantro, and red pepper. Set aside. In a small bowl, stir together yogurt, mayonnaise chipotle, and adobo. Stir sauce into chicken mixture until well combined. Chill covered for 1 hour to develop flavors. Serve in avocado halves. Makes 6 servings.

Chicken Caesar Salad

1 cup reduced-sodium chicken broth
2½ tablespoons grated Parmesan
1 tablespoon olive oil
1 teaspoon Dijon mustard
2 cloves garlic, minced
1 teaspoon anchovy paste
6 cups chopped Romaine lettuce
2 cups cooked chicken, cut into 1-inch cubes or shredded
1 cup cherry or grape tomatoes
1 cup herb-seasoned croutons

In a blender, combine chicken broth, Parmesan, olive oil, mustard, garlic, and anchovy paste. Purée until smooth and blended. Transfer lettuce to a large bowl, and top with chicken, tomatoes and croutons. Pour dressing over salad just before serving. Makes 6 servings.

Chicken Club Salad

3 cups cubed Italian bread
3 tablespoons olive oil
Salt and black pepper, to taste
3 pounds boneless, skinless chicken breasts, poached and cubed
1 pint cherry tomatoes, quartered
4 scallions, minced
6 slices lean bacon, cooked, drained, and crumbled
½ cup mayonnaise
Basil sprigs, for garnish

In a bowl, drizzle the bread cubes with the oil, tossing to coat evenly, and season with salt and pepper. Spread the bread cubes in a baking pan bake at 350° for 15 to 20 minutes until golden, and let cool.

In a large bowl, combine the chicken, tomatoes, scallions, two-thirds of the bacon, the mayonnaise, and salt and pepper. Divide the salad among plates, and arrange the croutons around it. Garnish each serving with some of the remaining bacon and a basil sprig. Makes 6 servings.

Chicken Noodle Salad with Peanut Ginger Dressing

⅓ cup smooth peanut butter
¼ cup soy sauce
2 tablespoons unseasoned rice vinegar
1 tablespoon Asian garlic chile sauce
1 tablespoon brown sugar, packed
1 tablespoon finely chopped fresh ginger
⅛ teaspoon red pepper flakes
3 tablespoons low-sodium chicken broth
Salt and black pepper, to taste
1 (16-ounce) package dried linguine, cooked al dente and drained
3½ cups cooked chicken, cut into strips
1 cup julienne carrot
6 green onions, chopped
1 red bell pepper, seeded and cut into strips
1 celery rib, thinly sliced
½ cup chopped fresh cilantro leaves
½ cup chopped roasted peanuts, for garnish

Place the peanut butter, soy sauce, rice vinegar, chile sauce, brown sugar, ginger, red pepper flakes, and chicken broth in a blender or food processor. Blend until smooth. Season to taste with salt and pepper. Thin the dressing to your taste by adding more chicken broth or water.

Place pasta in a large mixing bowl. Add chicken, carrots, green onions, bell pepper, celery, and cilantro. Pour dressing over and toss until mixture is evenly coated. Divide the salad among plates, and sprinkle with peanuts. Makes 8 servings.

Chicken Pasta Salad

½ cup nonfat mayonnaise
3 tablespoons low-sodium soy sauce
1 tablespoon white vinegar
⅛ teaspoon ground ginger
¼ teaspoon black pepper
1 cup dried spiral pasta, cooked and drained
2 cups cooked chicken breasts, cut into bite-size pieces
2 cups fresh snow peas, strings removed and blanched
2 green onions, sliced
½ cup sliced water chestnuts
¼ cup toasted almonds, for garnish

In a small bowl, combine the mayonnaise, soy sauce, vinegar, ginger, and pepper. Set aside. In a separate bowl, combine pasta, chicken, snow peas, green onions, and water chestnuts; toss with dressing mix. Refrigerate overnight. Sprinkle with toasted almonds before serving. Makes 4 servings.

Chicken Salad with Apples and Almonds

3 tablespoons nonfat sour cream
1 tablespoon reduced-calorie mayonnaise
Dash ground celery seed
Dash ground cardamom
⅛ teaspoon salt or to taste (optional)
1 cup roasted chicken breast cubes
1 cup cubed tart or sweet apple, peeled or unpeeled
1 small celery stalk, diced
2 tablespoons sliced almonds, toasted in skillet

In a medium bowl, stir together sour cream, mayonnaise, celery seed, cardamom, and salt, if desired. Stir in chicken, apple, celery, and almonds. Makes 4 servings.

Chicken Salad with Ranch Dressing

4 boneless, skinless chicken breasts, poached and diced
Salt and black pepper, to taste
½ cup diced celery
2 tablespoons chopped onion
1 tablespoon slivered almonds
¼ cup nonfat ranch salad dressing
Lettuce

Season chicken with salt and pepper. In a large bowl, combine chicken, celery, onion, almonds, and ranch dressing. Mix and serve on a cold bed of lettuce. Makes 4 servings.

Cold Peanut, Chicken, and Soba Noodle Salad

12 ounces dried soba noodles, cooked and drained
3 tablespoons sesame oil, divided
¼ cup chopped green onion, divided
1 jalapeño, seeded and minced
1 teaspoon minced garlic
1 teaspoon minced fresh ginger
½ cup creamy peanut butter
¼ cup soy sauce
¼ cup chicken broth
¼ cup chopped fresh cilantro
2 tablespoons fish sauce
1 tablespoon rice vinegar
2 tablespoons fresh lime juice
1 teaspoons sugar
½ teaspoon red pepper flakes
8 ounces boneless, skinless chicken breast, cut into strips and poached
½ cup chopped red bell pepper
1 cucumber, peeled, seeded, and chopped
2 tablespoons chopped roasted unsalted peanuts

In a large bowl, toss noodles with 1 tablespoon sesame oil, cover, and refrigerate. In a food processor, combine 2 tablespoons green onion, jalapeño, garlic, and ginger, and process on high speed. Add the remaining 2 tablespoons of sesame oil, peanut butter, soy sauce, chicken broth, cilantro, fish sauce, vinegar, lime juice, sugar, and pepper flakes. Toss the sauce with the noodles. To serve, toss the noodles with the chicken strips, bell pepper, cucumber, peanuts, and remaining green onion. Makes 2 servings.

Creamy Tarragon Chicken Salad

2 pounds boneless, skinless chicken breasts
1 cup chicken broth
⅓ cup chopped walnuts
⅔ cup sour cream
½ cup mayonnaise
1 tablespoon dried tarragon
½ teaspoon salt
½ teaspoon black pepper
1½ cups diced celery
1½ cups halved red seedless grapes

Arrange chicken in a glass baking dish large enough to hold it in a single layer. Pour broth around the chicken and bake at 450° until no longer pink in the center, 30 to 35 minutes. Transfer chicken to a cutting board until cool enough to handle, and cut into cubes. Meanwhile, spread walnuts on a baking sheet, toast in the oven until lightly golden and fragrant, about 6 minutes and let cool. Combine sour cream, mayonnaise, tarragon, and salt and pepper in a large bowl. Add celery, grapes, chicken, and walnuts; stir to combine. Makes 8 servings.

Curried Chicken and Peach Salad

6 tablespoons fat-free mayonnaise
6 tablespoons fat-free sour cream
¾ teaspoon sugar
¾ teaspoon lemon juice
½ teaspoon curry powder
⅛ teaspoon ground ginger
⅛ teaspoon ground cinnamon
8 cups torn Bibb lettuce
2 cups cooked and cubed chicken
3 cups peeled and sliced peaches
16 leaves Bibb lettuce
2 tablespoons pine nuts

Combine mayonnaise, sour cream, sugar, lemon juice, curry powder, ginger, and cinnamon. Add the torn lettuce, chicken, and peaches, and toss. Place 4 lettuce leaves on each plate, spoon 2 cups of salad mixture on it, and sprinkle with ½ tablespoon of pine nuts. Makes 4 servings.

Dijon Chicken Salad

1 cup low-sodium chicken broth
1 (4-ounce) package lemon-flavored sugar-free gelatin
¾ cup cold water
1 tablespoon red vinegar
¼ teaspoon black pepper
¼ cup plain low-fat yogurt
2 tablespoons low-fat sour cream
1 tablespoon Dijon mustard
1 cup finely chopped cooked chicken breast
1 cup finely chopped celery
½ cup chopped green or red bell pepper

Bring chicken broth to a boil in small saucepan. Completely dissolve gelatin in boiling broth. Add water, vinegar, and black pepper. Chill until slightly thickened. Stir in yogurt, sour cream, and mustard. Chill until slightly thickened. Stir in remaining ingredients. Spoon into ramekins or molds, and chill until firm, about 2 hours. Makes 4 servings.

Dill Lemon Chicken Pasta Salad

5 pounds boneless, skinless chicken breasts, cooked and cut into pieces
1 celery stalk, chopped
2 pounds lemon penne pasta
3 cups mayonnaise
⅓ cup lemon juice
½ teaspoon dried dill weed
1 cup buttermilk

In a large bowl, toss together chicken, celery, and pasta. In a separate large bowl, combine the mayonnaise, lemon juice, and dill weed. Mix well and stir in buttermilk. Add mayonnaise to chicken mixture, and toss to coat. Cover and chill for 20 minutes. Makes 10 servings.

Fruited Curry Chicken Salad

4 boneless, skinless chicken breasts, cooked and diced
1 celery stalk, chopped
½ onion, chopped
1 small apple, peeled, cored and chopped
⅓ cup golden raisins
⅓ cup halved seedless green grapes
½ cup chopped toasted pecans
⅛ teaspoon ground black pepper
½ teaspoon curry powder
¾ cup mayonnaise

In a large bowl, mix together all ingredients, tossing to coat. Makes 4 servings.

Fruity Chicken Salad with Pineapple

3 cups cooked, cubed chicken breast
1 celery stalk, chopped
1 (20-ounce) can pineapple chunks, drained
1 (11-ounce) can mandarin oranges, drained
¾ cup halved red or green seedless grapes
¼ cup chopped walnuts or pecans
¼ cup plain nonfat or low-fat yogurt
1 tablespoon nonfat or low-fat mayonnaise
1 tablespoon lemon juice

In a large bowl, combine chicken, celery, pineapple, oranges, grapes, and nuts. In a small bowl, mix yogurt, mayonnaise, and lemon juice with a fork. Add the dressing to the chicken mixture, and gently toss. Makes 6 servings.

Fruity Chicken Salad with Strawberries and Kiwi

2 tablespoons nonfat mayonnaise
2 tablespoons nonfat sour cream
¼ cup orange juice
2 boneless, skinless chicken breasts, cooked and cubed
1 cup sliced strawberries
2 kiwis, sliced
⅔ cup canned mandarin oranges, drained
8 lettuce leaves
3 tablespoons chopped cashews

Combine mayonnaise, sour cream, and orange juice in a large bowl. Add chicken, strawberries, kiwi, and oranges, and toss gently to coat. Cover and refrigerate for 2 hours. Serve on lettuce leaves, topped with cashews. Makes 8 servings.

Grandma's Chicken Salad

1 (2½- to 3-pound) chicken, cooked and coarsely chopped
2 cups chopped celery
¼ cup finely chopped green bell pepper
1 cup sweet pickle relish
6 hard-boiled eggs, chopped
1½ cups mayonnaise
1 teaspoon fresh lemon juice

Combine chicken, celery, bell pepper, relish, and eggs in a bowl. Add mayonnaise and lemon juice; mix gently. Chill until ready to serve. Makes 8 servings.

Greek Chicken Pasta Salad

½ cup chicken broth
1 tablespoon olive oil
1 tablespoon red vinegar
2 garlic cloves, minced
1 teaspoon Dijon mustard
1 teaspoon dried oregano
1 teaspoon dried thyme
Salt and black pepper, to taste
2 cups cooked, cubed chicken breasts
1 green bell pepper, seeded and diced
¼ cup chopped fresh mint leaves
12 ounces dried pasta, cooked according to package instructions and
  drained
½ cup crumbled feta cheese

In a small bowl, whisk together broth, oil, vinegar, garlic, mustard, oregano, thyme, and salt and pepper. Add chicken, green pepper, and mint. Add cooked pasta to bowl with dressing and chicken. Toss to combine. Cover and refrigerate. Top with feta cheese just before serving. Makes 4 servings.

Grilled Chicken and Asparagus Salad

1 pound boneless, skinless chicken breast
1 pound fresh asparagus, trimmed
10 ounces mixed baby greens
1 cup halved grape tomatoes
½ cup canned corn
½ cup crumbled feta cheese
⅓ cup sliced almonds, toasted
½ cup reduced-fat vinaigrette dressing

Grill chicken and asparagus over medium heat for 5 to 6 minutes per side, or until chicken is no longer pink and asparagus is tender. Remove from grill; slice into bite-sized pieces. In a large bowl, toss together greens, tomatoes, corn, feta cheese, and almonds. Top with the chicken and asparagus and drizzle with the dressing. Makes 4 servings.

Grilled Chicken Salad with Raspberry Vinaigrette

¼ cup raspberry vinegar
½ teaspoon dried basil
¼ teaspoon garlic powder
1 tablespoon olive oil
¼ teaspoon sugar
½ teaspoon salt
8 cups torn mixed salad greens
4 boneless, skinless chicken breasts, grilled and sliced

Combine vinegar, basil, garlic powder, olive oil, sugar, and salt in a jar. Cover tightly and shake vigorously. Pour vinegar mixture over greens, and toss gently. Divide among plates, and top with chicken. Makes 4 servings.

Grilled Pineapple and Chicken Salad

4 boneless, skinless chicken breasts
1 tablespoon olive oil, divided
Salt and black pepper, to taste
1 whole pineapple
¼ cup walnut oil
1 tablespoon chopped fresh chervil
½ cup minced celery
½ cup chopped roasted walnuts
1 teaspoon finely chopped parsley

Season chicken with salt, pepper, and ½ tablespoon of olive oil. Grill for about 4 minutes on each side. Let cool and cut into cubes.

Using a sharp knife, split pineapple in half. Make a slit around the sides, leaving about ¼-inch trim, and remove fruit. Reserve pineapple boats, if desired. Remove core of pineapple, and cut fruit into ½-inch slices. Season slices with salt, pepper, and remaining olive oil. Grill for 1 to 2 minutes on each side. Let cool. Reserve 2 slices of the pineapples, and dice the rest of the fruit.

In a mixing bowl, add the two reserved slices of fruit. Using the back of a fork, mash fruit against side of bowl. Add walnut oil and whisk until emulsified. Stir in the chervil and season with salt and pepper. In a mixing bowl, toss the diced chicken, pineapple, celery, and walnuts with the dressing. Cover and refrigerate for 1 hour. Serve in pineapple boats, garnished with chopped parsley. Makes 4 servings.

Honey Mustard Chicken Salad

4 ounces canned low-sodium white chicken, drained
¼ teaspoon grated fresh lemon zest
2 tablespoons nonfat honey mustard salad dressing
¼ cup chopped water chestnuts
½ cup halved seedless red grapes
1 teaspoon pine nuts, toasted in a skillet
1 cup fresh spinach, washed, dried, and stems removed
Black pepper, to taste

Toss chicken, lemon zest, salad dressing, water chestnuts, and grapes together in a small bowl, until all ingredients are lightly coated. Let salad stand for 5 minutes to absorb dressing. Arrange the spinach on a plate. Place the salad on top of the spinach. Sprinkle with pine nuts and black pepper. Makes 4 servings.

Hot Chicken Salad

2 cups cooked, cubed chicken breast
1½ cups diced celery
½ cup chopped nuts
1 cup mayonnaise
2 tablespoons lemon juice
½ teaspoon salt
½ cup grated American or Cheddar cheese
1 cup finely crushed potato chips

Combine chicken, celery, nuts, mayonnaise, lemon juice, and salt. Heat thoroughly. Pile into small casserole. Sprinkle with grated cheese, and top with crushed potato chips. Bake at 400° for 10 minutes or until brown. Makes 4 servings.

Italian Chicken Salad

10 cups coarsely shredded cooked chicken
**2 cups roasted red and yellow bell peppers, drained, patted dry, and
  coarsely chopped**
1¼ cups thinly sliced red onion
¾ cup chopped fresh Italian parsley
¾ cup slivered almonds, toasted
½ cup drained capers
1½ cups vinaigrette dressing
Salt and freshly ground black pepper, to taste
20 butter lettuce leaves
1 (4-ounce) piece Parmesan, shaved with vegetable peeler

Toss the chicken, bell peppers, onion, parsley, almonds, and capers in a large
bowl with enough vinaigrette to moisten. Season the chicken salad with salt
and black pepper. Arrange 1 large lettuce cup and 1 small lettuce cup on
each plate, overlapping slightly. Spoon the chicken salad into the lettuce
cups. Drizzle more vinaigrette over the salads, and sprinkle with Parmesan.
Makes 10 servings.

Macaroni Salad with Creamy Dill Dressing

2 cups cooked, cubed chicken
4 cups cooked elbow macaroni
1 cup frozen cooked small shrimp, thawed
1 celery stalk, chopped
¼ cup chopped onion
¼ cup chopped green bell pepper
¼ cup chopped red bell pepper
½ cup shredded low-fat Cheddar cheese
⅓ cup nonfat sour cream
⅓ cup reduced-calorie mayonnaise
4 teaspoons red vinegar
1 teaspoon snipped fresh dill
¼ teaspoon black pepper
¼ teaspoon sugar

In a bowl, combine the first 8 ingredients. In another bowl, combine the remaining ingredients. Stir well. Pour over salad, and toss to coat. Cover and chill for several hours. Makes 4 servings.

Old-Fashioned Chicken Salad

2 cups chicken, cooked and chopped
2 eggs, hard-boiled and chopped
1½ cups celery, diced
½ cup sweet pickles, chopped
½ cup mayonnaise
1 teaspoon salt
⅛ teaspoon pepper

Combine chicken, eggs, celery, and pickles; mix well. Add mayonnaise, salt, and pepper. Mix thoroughly and chill. Makes 4 servings.

Parisian Chicken Salad

4 cups mixed baby greens, rinsed and patted dry
1 cup sliced mushrooms
1 cup diced fennel
1 cup julienned carrots
1 cup diced celery
1 (14-ounce) can baby artichokes, drained and quartered
1 cup Kalamata or Niçoise olives
½ cup thinly sliced scallion
2 boneless, skinless chicken breasts, pounded to ½-inch thickness
1 tablespoon minced fresh thyme, or 1 teaspoon dried thyme
Salt and black pepper, to taste
1 tablespoon olive oil
1 cup chicken broth
1 to 2 teaspoons Dijon mustard, or to taste
2 to 3 tablespoons olive oil, or to taste
1 tablespoon balsamic vinegar

In a large salad bowl, combine greens, mushrooms, fennel, carrots, celery, artichokes, olives, and scallion, and toss. Pat chicken dry and season with thyme, salt, and pepper. In a large nonstick skillet set over moderately high heat, warm 1 tablespoon oil until hot, add the chicken, and sauté it for 2 minutes. Turn and cook for 1 minute more. Add broth, and whisk in mustard. Simmer 2 to 3 minutes, or until the chicken is cooked through. Transfer chicken to a plate, reduce the remaining liquid to ½ cup, and pour it into a small bowl. Whisk the olive oil into the cooking liquid, and then and whisk in the vinegar, salt, and black pepper. Cut chicken into slices and add to the salad bowl. Pour juices from plate into dressing, whisking to combine, and drizzle over salad. Toss mixture until chicken and vegetables are well coated with dressing. Makes 4 servings.

Parmesan and Basil Chicken Salad

1 cup mayonnaise
1 cup chopped fresh basil
2 garlic cloves, crushed
3 celery stalks, chopped
Salt and black pepper, to taste
2 boneless, skinless chicken breasts, roasted and cubed
⅔ cup grated Parmesan cheese

In a food processor, purée mayonnaise, basil, garlic, and celery. Season with salt and pepper. Combine the chicken, puréed mixture, and Parmesan cheese; toss and refrigerate. Makes 2 servings.

Pecos Chicken and Cornbread Salad

1 package cornbread mix
1 (4½-ounce) can chopped green chiles
1 tablespoon vegetable oil
4 boneless, skinless chicken breasts, cut in ½-inch cubes
1 (10-ounce) can tomatoes with mild green chiles, drained and diced
1 teaspoon ground cumin
½ teaspoon chili powder
3 cups thinly sliced romaine lettuce
1 (11-ounce) can whole-kernel corn, drained
1 (15-ounce) can red kidney beans, rinsed and drained
1 cup finely diced green peppers
1 cup finely diced red onions
1 cup sour cream
1 cup mayonnaise
2 cups shredded Cheddar cheese, divided

Mix cornbread batter as directed, stirring in the can of chopped green chiles. Pour the batter into a medium pan, and bake according to the package directions. Remove the cornbread from the oven, cool, and cut into 1-inch cubes.

While the cornbread is baking, heat a small amount of oil in a heavy skillet over medium-high heat. Add the chicken and tomatoes; bring to a quick boil, and stir in the spices. Cover and simmer the chicken mixture for 5 minutes; remove from heat and cool. Wait until the cornbread and the chicken mixture are completely cool before assembling the salad.

In a large glass bowl, layer the following ingredients: half of the cornbread, half of the chicken mixture, half of the lettuce, and half of each of the vegetables. In a small bowl, combine the sour cream and mayonnaise. Spread half of this mixture over the vegetables and sprinkle with half of the Cheddar cheese. Repeat this process, ending with the Cheddar cheese. Cover and chill for at least 2 hours before serving. Makes 10 to 12 servings.

Raspberry Chicken Salad

¼ cup raspberry preserves
2 tablespoons olive oil
1 tablespoon white vinegar
1 teaspoon Dijon mustard
Salt and black pepper, to taste
2 tablespoons minced scallion
1 cup fresh raspberries
4 boneless, skinless chicken breasts, cooked and cut into 1-inch pieces
4 cups chopped Bibb lettuce
Nut bread and cream cheese (optional)

In a medium bowl, whisk together preserves, oil, vinegar, mustard, salt, and pepper. Add scallions and raspberries to vinaigrette. Add chicken and toss to combine with vinaigrette. Arrange lettuce on individual plates and top with chicken mixture. Serve with nut bread and cream cheese, if desired. Makes 4 servings.

Simple Southwestern Chicken Salad

2 boneless, skinless chicken breasts, cooked and cubed
¾ cup mayonnaise
¼ cup chopped celery
2 tablespoons fresh chopped cilantro
1 (1-ounce) package taco seasoning mix

In a medium bowl, combine ingredients and mix well. Cover and refrigerate for 1 hour. Makes 2 servings.

Spicy Chicken Pasta Salad

1 cup oil-packed sun-dried tomatoes, drained
1 medium onion, chopped
1 red bell pepper, chopped
1 yellow bell pepper, chopped
1 green bell pepper, chopped
1 to 2 tablespoons olive oil
2 pounds boneless, skinless chicken breasts, cooked and cut into strips
12 to 16 ounces dried bowtie pasta, cooked
1 (12-ounce) bottle balsamic vinaigrette
1 cup freshly grated Parmesan cheese

Sauté tomatoes, onion, and peppers in skillet with olive oil. Combine sautéed vegetables, chicken, and pasta in a serving dish. Add vinaigrette and toss. Top with cheese. Makes 4 to 6 servings.

Sunflower Chicken Salad

2 cups cooked, cubed chicken breast
1 cup cubed Cheddar cheese
¼ cup sunflower seeds
¼ cup thinly sliced celery
½ cup halved seedless green grapes
½ cup mayonnaise
Salt and black pepper, to taste
Rolls or lettuce leaves (optional)

In a large bowl combine ingredients and mix well. Serve on rolls or lettuce leaves, if desired. Makes 4 servings.

Wild Rice Salad

1 cup uncooked wild rice
Salt or seasoned salt (optional)
2 cups cooked, diced chicken
1½ cups halved seedless green grapes
1 cup sliced water chestnuts
¾ cup reduced-calorie mayonnaise
1 cup cashews (optional)
Lettuce leaves

Cook rice according to package directions, omitting salt or substituting seasoned salt, if desired. Drain well; cool to room temperature. Place rice into a large bowl; add chicken, grapes, water chestnuts, and mayonnaise. Toss gently with a fork. Cover and chill. Just before serving, add cashews, if desired. Serve on lettuce leaves, or line a bowl with lettuce leaves, and fill with salad. Makes 4 servings.

Winesap Apple Pesto Chicken Salad

3 grilled chicken breasts
Salt and black pepper, to taste
½ cup julienned red bell pepper
½ cup julienned red onion
2 Winesap apples, cored, peeled, quartered, and sliced
¼ cup low-fat mayonnaise
¼ cup pesto
Bibb lettuce
Endive

Season chicken with salt and pepper. Refrigerate until cooled. Once cooled, julienne chicken breasts. In a mixing bowl, combine chicken, red pepper, red onion, and apples. In a separate bowl, combine mayonnaise and pesto. Combine the chicken and pesto mixtures. Serve on a bed of Bibb lettuce and endive. Makes 3 servings.

SOUPS AND
STEWS

Brunswick Stew

1 teaspoon olive oil, divided
1 large sweet onion, diced
3 celery stalks, cut into ¼-inch slices
3 ounces Canadian bacon, cut into ¼-inch slices
1 red bell pepper, cut into ¼-inch slices
2 boneless skinless chicken breasts and 2 hindquarters, cut into 1½-inch chunks
2 cups canned crushed tomatoes
1 cup low-sodium chicken broth
1 tablespoon Worcestershire sauce
¼ teaspoon cayenne pepper
1 cup frozen baby lima beans
1 cup frozen corn kernels
1 tablespoon arrowroot mixed with 2 tablespoons stock or water
¼ cup chopped fresh parsley
¼ cup chopped fresh basil

Heat ½ teaspoon of the oil in a 10½-inch pan on medium high. Sauté onion 3 minutes, or until it starts to turn translucent. Add celery, Canadian bacon, and red bell pepper, and cook 3 more minutes. Remove to a plate. Without washing pan, add remaining ½ teaspoon oil, and heat. When the pan is hot, toss in chicken and brown for 2 minutes. Pour in tomatoes, broth, and Worcestershire sauce. Add cooked vegetables and cayenne. Bring to a boil, reduce heat, cover, and simmer for 35 minutes, or until chicken is tender. Add lima beans and corn, and cook for 12 minutes more, or until beans are tender. Stir in arrowroot, and heat to thicken. Garnish with parsley and basil. Makes 8 servings.

Caribbean Stewed Chicken

3 pounds skinless chicken pieces
1 large onion, chopped
1 large tomato, coarsely chopped
2 tablespoons fresh lemon juice
1 tablespoon chopped fresh parsley
½ teaspoon dried thyme
½ teaspoon dried rosemary
¼ teaspoon ground ginger
¼ teaspoon ground cinnamon
3 cups water
1 tablespoon salt (optional)
¼ teaspoon freshly ground black pepper
1 tablespoon margarine
2 tablespoons all-purpose flour
¼ teaspoon ground nutmeg

Place chicken, onion, tomato, lemon juice, parsley, thyme, rosemary, ginger, and cinnamon in a glass bowl; cover and let stand in refrigerator for 2 hours to marinate. Transfer to a Dutch oven or stewing pot; add water, salt, and pepper. Cover and bring to a boil; reduce heat and simmer 1½ hours or until tender (start checking after 1 hour). Remove chicken and strain broth into a bowl. Melt margarine in a small saucepan; stir in flour and nutmeg until blended. Remove and add 1½ cups chicken broth to flour mixture; stir for about 2 minutes until thickened. Place chicken pieces on a warm platter; serve with sauce. Reserve remaining broth for later use. Makes 8 servings.

Cheesy Chicken Soup

3 cups chopped roasted chicken
1 (16-ounce) can chicken broth
½ teaspoon all-purpose seasoning
½ teaspoon Italian seasoning
1 cup shredded sharp Cheddar cheese

Combine all ingredients except cheese in a pot and bring to boil. Add cheese a little bit at a time while stirring as it melts. Makes 3 servings.

Chicken and Bacon Corn Chowder

½ pound thick bacon, diced
1 tablespoon extra-virgin olive oil
5 stalks celery, diced
2 medium Spanish onions, diced
2 medium russet or all-purpose potatoes, peeled and diced
8 ears fresh corn kernels, removed from cob
1 to 2 teaspoons fresh thyme leaves
1½ quarts chicken broth
3 cups heavy cream
2½ pounds boneless, skinless chicken breast, cooked and shredded
Salt and black pepper, to taste

Heat bacon and olive oil in a large pot over medium heat. Cook until bacon fat is rendered and meat is firming but not yet crisp, about 5 minutes. Add celery and onions. Reduce heat to medium-low; cook, stirring occasionally until vegetables begin to soften, about 6 minutes. Add potatoes, corn, and thyme. Continue to cook, stirring occasionally, until onions are fully soft, about 8 additional minutes.

Add chicken broth to the pot. Bring to a simmer over medium-high heat. Turn down the heat to medium and simmer until potatoes are tender, about 10 minutes. Add the cream and shredded chicken. Return chowder to a simmer, and season to taste with salt and pepper. Makes 6 servings.

Chicken and Chickpea Soup

1 cup chickpeas
1 onion, peeled and halved
1 bay leaf
2 tablespoons olive oil
3 boneless chicken thighs with skin, each cut in half
Salt and black pepper, to taste
2 ounces bacon, diced
1 onion, chopped
3 garlic cloves, minced or pureed
1 generous pinch saffron threads
½ cup chicken broth
2 carrots, peeled and sliced ½-inch thick
2 ribs celery, sliced ½-inch thick
2 cups chopped cabbage
2 teaspoons salt
½ teaspoon freshly ground pepper
6 cups stock or water
½ bunch fresh parsley, chopped

Place chickpeas in large saucepan with enough water to cover by several inches. Add onion halves and bay leaf. Bring to a boil, lower heat to a simmer, and cook 1 hour, until about done.

In the meantime, heat oil in large Dutch oven over medium-high heat. Season chicken thighs with salt and pepper, and place chicken pieces, skin-side down, in hot pot. Cook until evenly golden brown, about 5 minutes, then flip over and cook other side 5 minutes. Remove chicken and set aside. Pour off all but 2 tablespoons fat from the pan, and add bacon. Cook 5 minutes until crisp. Drain excess fat. Add chopped onion, garlic, and saffron, and stir. Cook until onions start to soften; add broth and scrape bottom of the pot to loosen any browned bits. Add carrots, celery, cabbage, salt and pepper.

Remove onion halves from chickpeas, and add half-cooked chickpeas and their cooking liquid to pot along with the 6 cups of stock or water. Bring pot to a boil, lower heat, and simmer 45 to 60 minutes, or until chicken and chickpeas are completely cooked. Stir in parsley and serve. Makes 8 servings.

Chicken and Corn Soup

½ stewing hen
2 quarts chicken broth
¼ cup coarsely chopped onion
½ cup coarsely chopped carrots
½ cup coarsely chopped celery
1 teaspoon saffron threads (optional)
¾ cup corn kernels, fresh or frozen
½ cup minced celery
1 tablespoon chopped fresh parsley
1 cup dried egg noodles, cooked and drained

Combine stewing hen with chicken broth, onions, carrots, celery, and saffron threads. Bring the stock to a simmer. Simmer for about 1 hour, skimming the surface as necessary. Remove and reserve hen until cool enough to handle; pick the meat from the bones and cut into neat little pieces. Strain the saffron broth through a fine sieve. Add corn, minced celery, parsley, and cooked noodles to the broth. Return soup to a simmer, and serve immediately. Makes 8 servings.

Chicken and Mushroom Stew

1 (3-pound) chicken, cut into serving-sized pieces
8 cups boiling water
2 tablespoons vegetable oil
½ small onion, thinly sliced
2 celery stalks, thinly sliced
1 carrot, thinly sliced
1 bay leaf
½ teaspoon black pepper
8 ounces fresh mushrooms, sliced
2 tablespoons butter
2 teaspoons salt
½ cup instant rice

Brown chicken in hot oil; cover with boiling water. Add onion, bay leaf, celery, carrot, and pepper. In large skillet, brown mushrooms in butter until dry, and add to chicken. After 30 minutes, add salt and rice, and cook 20 more minutes. Makes 8 servings.

Chicken and Rice Soup

3 pounds chicken pieces
8 cups water
½ cup chopped celery with leaves
¼ cup chopped fresh parsley
1 small onion, quartered
Dash black pepper
1 bay leaf
¼ teaspoon celery seeds
½ cup uncooked rice
1 cup diced carrots

Simmer chicken in water with celery, parsley, onion, pepper, bay leaf, and celery seeds for 4 hours in a slow cooker or 1 hour over low heat on the stove. Drain chicken broth and remove chicken pieces (discard bay leaf). Pick the meat from the chicken, and chop into bite-size pieces. Combine broth, chicken, rice, and carrots in a saucepan. Cook for 30 to 40 minutes, or until the rice is tender. Makes 8 servings.

Chicken and Sausage Gumbo

4 boneless, skinless chicken breasts and thighs, cut into small chunks
½ teaspoon Creole seasoning blend
3 tablespoons all-purpose flour
1 tablespoon vegetable oil
2 cups smoked sausage, cut in ½-inch pieces
½ cup vegetable oil
½ cup all-purpose flour
1 cup chopped onion
½ cup chopped green bell pepper
¼ cup chopped red bell pepper
3 ribs celery, chopped
3 medium garlic cloves, minced
1 (14½-ounce) can diced tomatoes
1 small bay leaf
6 cups chicken broth
1 teaspoon Creole seasoning blend, or to taste
½ teaspoon dried thyme leaves
Salt and freshly ground black pepper to taste
4 green onions, chopped
2 tablespoons fresh parsley, chopped

Sprinkle chicken with Creole seasoning, and toss with flour. Heat 1 tablespoon oil in a heavy skillet over medium heat; add chicken. Cook, stirring, until browned. Transfer to a dish, and set aside. Brown sliced sausage; add to chicken mixture.

In a heavy pot, heat ½ cup oil; add ½ cup flour. Cook, stirring constantly, until the roux reaches a deep golden color. Add vegetables and stir briskly. Continue to cook, stirring constantly, for about 3 to 4 minutes.

Add the chicken broth, seasonings, chicken, and sausage. Bring to a boil, then cook for about 1 to 1½ hours, skimming excess fat off the top several times, as needed. Add the chopped green onions and parsley; heat for 5 to 10 minutes longer. Mound hot cooked rice in bowls, ladle gumbo around the mound, and serve with crusty bread and butter. Makes 6 servings.

Chicken Barley Soup

1 (3-pound) chicken, cut into pieces
9 cups water
3 celery stalks, chopped, leaves reserved
1 small onion, quartered
½ cup finely chopped carrot
½ cup chopped onion
½ cup chopped fresh parsley
½ cup uncooked barley
2 tablespoons fresh lemon juice
1 tablespoon salt
½ teaspoon black pepper
¼ teaspoon celery seed
1½ cups fresh green beans, cut into 1-inch pieces

Place chicken, water, leaves from celery, and small onion in a large saucepan. Cover and bring to a boil. Reduce heat and simmer 1½ hours, until chicken is tender. Remove chicken and strain broth into a bowl. Chill until fat sets on top. Remove fat. Remove skin and bones from chicken; discard. Cut chicken into bite-size pieces; set aside. (Note: if you want less than 8 servings, freeze extra broth and chicken separately in meal-sized portions.) Return broth to saucepan. Add chopped celery, carrot, onion, parsley, barley, lemon juice, and seasonings. Cover and simmer 20 minutes. Add fresh green beans and chicken. Continue cooking for 15 minutes, or until beans are tender. Makes 8 servings.

Chicken Carbonara Soup

2 eggs
1 cup dried spaghetti, broken into smaller pieces and cooked according
   to package directions
4 tablespoons extra-virgin olive oil, divided
1 cup cooked, diced chicken breast
½ cup frozen peas, thawed and drained
3 green onions, thinly sliced
¾ cup heavy whipping cream
1½ cups low-sodium chicken stock
3 ounces shaved Parmesan cheese
8 slices cooked bacon, chopped
1 teaspoon minced garlic
1 tablespoon fresh chopped parsley
2 teaspoons black pepper

In a large bowl, beat two eggs until frothy. Pour cooked spaghetti into bowl of eggs and immediately begin tossing, the heat will cook the eggs. Toss with 1 tablespoon olive oil to prevent sticking. In a large saucepan, heat 3 tablespoons of olive oil. Add chicken, peas, and onions, and cook for a few minutes. Slowly add heavy cream, stirring constantly. Slowly add chicken stock, stirring again. Heat for another 5 minutes on low heat, being careful not to boil. Add cheese, spaghetti mixture, bacon, garlic, parsley, and pepper, mixing all ingredients until cheese has melted. Makes 2 servings.

Chicken Chili

2 pounds boneless, skinless chicken thighs
3 (14-ounce) cans diced tomatoes with chiles and garlic, undrained
1 (1-ounce) package taco seasoning mix
2 (15-ounce) cans pinto beans, drained and rinsed

Combine all ingredients in a slow cooker. Cover and cook on low for 7 to 9 hours, or until chicken is tender. Stir well so that the chicken breaks into small pieces. Makes 6 servings.

Chicken Chowder

½ cup chopped carrots
1 cup skim milk
1 cup low-sodium chicken broth
⅛ teaspoon white pepper
1 onion, chopped
2 garlic cloves, minced
1 potato, peeled and cubed
½ pound boneless, skinless chicken breasts, cut into 1-inch pieces
2 (15-ounce) cans creamed corn
¼ cup dried potato flakes
½ cup grated Parmesan cheese

Combine all ingredients except dried potato flakes and cheese in a slow cooker. Cover and cook on low for 5 to 6 hours, or until potatoes are tender and chicken is thoroughly cooked. Add potato flakes and stir well to combine. Cook mixture on high, uncovered, for 5 to 10 minutes, or until chowder has thickened and dried potato flakes have dissolved. Top each serving with cheese. Makes 4 servings.

Chicken Egg Soup

4 to 5 cups chicken broth
3 eggs
Salt and black pepper, to taste

Put the chicken broth into a pot, cover, and place over medium-high heat. When it is close to the simmering point, break eggs into a bowl and beat them. Pour in beaten eggs as soon as broth starts boiling, whisking soup while adding beaten egg. Season and serve immediately. Makes 4 to 6 servings.

Chicken, Mushroom, and Zucchini Stew

6 boneless, skinless chicken breasts, cut into 1-inch cubes
2 tablespoons cooking oil
1 cup sliced fresh mushrooms
1 medium onion, sliced
3 cups diced zucchini
1 cup diced green bell pepper
4 garlic cloves, minced
3 medium tomatoes, diced
1 (6-ounce) can tomato paste
¾ cup water
2 teaspoons salt
1 teaspoon dried thyme

Place ingredients in a slow cooker in the order listed. Cover and cook on low for 6 to 8 hours. Makes 6 to 8 servings.

Chicken Noodle Soup

2 tablespoons extra-virgin olive oil
1 medium onion, chopped
3 garlic cloves, minced
2 medium carrots, cut diagonally into ½-inch-thick slices
2 celery ribs, halved lengthwise and cut into ½-inch-thick slices
4 fresh thyme sprigs
1 bay leaf
2 quarts chicken stock
8 ounces dried wide egg noodles
1½ cups shredded cooked chicken
Kosher salt and freshly ground black pepper
1 handful fresh flat-leaf parsley, finely chopped

Place a soup pot over medium heat and coat with the oil. Add the onion, garlic, carrots, celery, thyme, and bay leaf. Cook and stir for about 6 minutes, until the vegetables are softened but not browned. Pour in the chicken stock and bring the liquid to a boil. Add the noodles and simmer for 5 minutes until tender. Fold in the chicken, and continue to simmer for another couple of minutes to heat through; season with salt and pepper. Sprinkle with chopped parsley before serving. Makes 4 servings.

Chicken Tarragon Soup

1 cup onion, chopped
½ cup sliced celery
1 garlic clove, crushed
2 tablespoons butter or margarine
2 (13¾-ounce) cans chicken broth
1 (8-ounce) can mixed vegetables
1 (14½-ounce) can Italian stewed tomatoes
1 cup diced cooked chicken
1 tablespoon dried parsley
¼ teaspoon dried tarragon

Sauté onion, celery, and garlic in butter 5 minutes. Add broth, mixed vegetables, tomatoes, chicken, parsley, and tarragon. Bring to boil; reduce heat. Cover and simmer 5 minutes. Makes 4 servings.

Chicken Tortilla Soup with Chipotle and Fire-Roasted Tomato

3 cups chicken stock
1 pound chicken tenders
1 bay leaf
1 tablespoon extra-virgin olive oil
4 slices thick, smoky center-cut bacon, chopped
1 onion, finely chopped
4 garlic cloves, chopped
2 chipotle peppers in adobo, chopped, plus 2 tablespoons sauce
1 (28-ounce) can crushed fire roasted tomatoes
Salt
4 cups lightly crushed corn tortilla chips
2 cups shredded fresh smoked mozzarella
1 lime, cut into wedges
½ red onion, chopped
Freshly chopped cilantro leaves, for garnish

Bring broth to a simmer, and add chicken tenders, poach 6 to 7 minutes with a bay leaf. While chicken poaches, heat extra-virgin olive oil in a medium soup pot or deep skillet over medium-high heat. Add bacon and cook until crisp, and remove with slotted spoon. Drain off excess fat, leaving 2 to 3 tablespoons in the pan. Add onions and garlic to the skillet, and cook 5 minutes. Stir in chipotles and tomatoes. Remove chicken from stock, dice, and then add to soup. Pass stock through a strainer, and add to the soup. Place 1 cup crushed tortilla chips in the bottom of each soup bowl. Cover with ½ cup smoked cheese. Ladle hot soup over the top. Serve with lime, onions, and cilantro. Makes 4 servings.

Colorful Chicken Stew

1 pound boneless skinless chicken breasts, cut into cubes
1 (14½-ounce) can Italian-style diced tomatoes, undrained
2 medium potatoes, peeled and cut into ½-inch cubes
5 medium carrots, chopped
3 celery stalks, chopped
1 large onion, chopped
1 medium green bell pepper, chopped
2 (4-ounce) cans mushroom stems and pieces, drained
2 low-sodium chicken bouillon cubes
2 teaspoons sugar
1 teaspoon chili powder
¼ teaspoon black pepper
1 tablespoon cornstarch
2 cups cold water

In a slow cooker, combine all ingredients except the cornstarch and the water. In a small bowl, combine cornstarch and water until smooth. Stir into chicken mixture. Cover and cook on low for 8 to 10 hours or until vegetables are tender. Makes 8 servings.

Country Chicken Stew

4½ cups chicken broth
3 pounds boneless, skinless chicken breasts, cut into cubes
1 cup diced sweet onion
1 tablespoon butter
½ cup all-purpose flour
2 tablespoons vegetable oil
2 cups frozen peas and carrots
Salt and black pepper, to taste

Place chicken broth, chicken, onions, and butter in a slow cooker. Cover and cook on high 1 hour. Whisk in flour. Add remaining ingredients, and cook on low for 5 to 7 hours. Makes 4 servings.

Creamy Walnut Chicken Soup

6 tablespoons unsalted butter
3 large onions, diced
4 tablespoons chopped garlic
2½ cups walnuts, toasted and divided
½ teaspoon hot paprika
1 teaspoon dried tarragon
1 teaspoon ground turmeric
2 teaspoons ground coriander
2 teaspoons salt
1 teaspoon black pepper
2 pounds boneless, skinless chicken breast, cut into 1-inch cubes
6 cups chicken broth
1 cup chopped fresh parsley
1 cup heavy cream
Sour cream

Heat butter over medium high in a large stockpot. Once foam subsides, add onions. Sauté until translucent and starting to turn golden brown, about 5 to 7 minutes. Add garlic and sauté for 3 more minutes. Turn heat down to medium, and add 2 cups walnuts, paprika, tarragon, turmeric, coriander, salt, and pepper. Add chicken and sauté until starting to brown, about 5 minutes. Add chicken broth and parsley, and simmer 10 minutes, or until chicken is cooked through. Remove pot from heat. Add heavy cream. Using an immersion blender, (or standard blender, working in batches) purée soup until smooth. Ladle into bowls. Top each bowl with sour cream and remaining walnuts. Makes 6 servings.

Creole Red Beans and Rice Soup

2 tablespoons olive oil
1 (4-pound) whole chicken, cut into 10 pieces
Creole seasoning
1½ cups chopped onions
1 cup chopped celery
1 cup diced carrots
1 tablespoon minced garlic
2 bay leaves
Dash crushed red pepper
1 (16-ounce) can red beans, rinsed and drained
1 gallon chicken stock
¼ pound long grain white rice, uncooked
½ cup chopped green onions

In a large stockpot, heat the olive oil. Season the chicken with Creole seasoning. When the oil is hot, add the chicken, sear for 4 to 5 minutes on each side. Add the onions, celery, and carrots. Season with Creole seasoning. Sauté the vegetables for 4 minutes. Add the garlic, bay leaves, pinch of crushed red pepper, and red beans and sauté for 1 minute. Add the stock and bring the liquid to a boil. Reduce the heat to a simmer, uncovered, for about 2 hours or until the beans are tender. Add the rice and continue to cook for 20 minutes or until the rice is tender. Remove from the heat and stir in the green onions. Makes 8 servings.

Easy Chicken Stew

1 (3-pound) chicken, cut into serving-sized pieces
8 cups boiling water
2 tablespoons vegetable oil
½ small onion, sliced
2 celery stalks, sliced
1 carrot, sliced
1 bay leaf
½ teaspoon black pepper
2 teaspoons salt

Brown chicken in hot oil; cover with boiling water. Add onion, bay leaf, celery, carrot, and pepper. After 30 minutes, add salt and cook 15 more minutes. Makes 8 servings.

Easy Mexican Chicken Soup

1 boil-in-bag rice packet
2 (14-ounce) cans low-fat, low-sodium chicken broth
8 ounces frozen cooked cubed chicken breast meat
1 (10½-ounce) can Mexican-style diced tomatoes with green chiles,
  drained
¼ cup chopped fresh cilantro
½ medium avocado, diced
1 to 2 medium limes, cut in wedges

In a medium saucepan, cook rice according to directions on package, omitting any salt or fats. When cooked, place rice in a separate bowl, and set aside. Discard water for rice, and add chicken broth to saucepan. Bring to a boil, add frozen chicken, and return just to a boil. Reduce heat and simmer for 2 minutes to heat chicken thoroughly. To serve, place ½ cup rice in the bottom of four individual shallow soup bowls, and spoon ¾ cup chicken around the mound of rice. Top rice with 2 tablespoons tomatoes and 1 tablespoon cilantro, and sprinkle 2 tablespoons avocado around sides. Squeeze lime over all. Makes 4 servings.

Fireside Chicken Soup

1 medium carrot, sliced
1 celery stalk, sliced
¾ cup sliced mushrooms
2 tablespoons butter or margarine
2 packages chicken-flavored ramen noodles
4 cups water, divided
1½ cups cooked, shredded chicken
2 tablespoons all-purpose flour
2 green onions, sliced
4 tablespoons grated Parmesan cheese
2 tablespoons finely chopped parsley

Sauté carrot, celery, and mushrooms in butter until tender. Add noodles with seasoning packets, 3½ cups water, and chicken. Cook for 3 minutes. Thoroughly combine flour and remaining ½ cup cold water. Stir into soup. Cook and stir until thickened. Stir in green onions. Garnish with cheese and parsley. Makes 2 servings.

Garden Soup

6 cups water
2 cups tomato juice
1 cup peeled and chopped potato
1 cup chopped onion
1 cup lima beans
¾ cup cooked and chopped chicken
½ cup sliced carrots
½ cup chopped celery
2 tablespoons chicken-flavored bouillon granules
1 teaspoon garlic powder
1½ teaspoons Worcestershire sauce

Combine all ingredients in a large Dutch oven. Cover and bring to a boil. Reduce heat and simmer for 45 minutes to 1 hour. Makes 4 servings.

Harvest Chicken Chowder

6 cups chicken broth
½ teaspoon salt
½ teaspoon freshly ground black pepper
6 medium potatoes, peeled and cubed
3 medium carrots, cut into cubes
¼ cup diced celery
½ cup finely chopped onion
2 pounds boneless, skinless chicken breasts, diced
1 (4-ounce) can sliced mushrooms, drained
1 cup frozen whole-kernel corn, thawed
1 (10¾-ounce) can cream of chicken soup
4 slices bacon, cooked crisp and crumbled
1 cup heavy whipping cream
3 tablespoons all-purpose flour
⅓ cup water
Parsley sprigs, for garnish

In a large pot, combine broth, salt, pepper, potatoes, carrots, celery, and onion. Bring to a boil over medium heat. Reduce heat to low. Cover and simmer for 30 minutes until carrots are tender. Stir in chicken, mushrooms, and corn. Cook over low heat for 10 to 15 minutes, until chicken is done, stirring often. Stir in cream of chicken soup, bacon, and cream. Heat through. In a small bowl, stir together flour and water until smooth. Stir into pot. Heat over low heat until chowder thickens slightly, stirring often. Ladle into bowls and garnish with parsley sprigs. Makes 8 servings.

Hearty Chicken and Asparagus Soup

1 tablespoon margarine
⅓ cup finely chopped onion
1 (14-ounce) can chicken broth
6 fresh asparagus tips
1½ cups milk
2 tablespoons cornstarch
3 ounces purchased honey-roasted chicken breast, cut into cubes
⅓ cup shredded Cheddar cheese

In a medium saucepan, melt margarine over low heat. Add onion and sauté for 4 minutes until light golden, stirring occasionally. Add the chicken broth and asparagus; raise heat to medium, and boil covered until asparagus is tender (approximately 10 minutes). In a small bowl, mix ½ cup milk with cornstarch until smooth. Slowly stir into saucepan. Stir in remaining milk, and continue to stir occasionally until mixture is thick. Stir in chicken and heat 1 minute more. Sprinkle cheese on top. Serve immediately. Makes 2 servings.

Home-Style Chicken Soup

3 onions, chopped
4 celery stalks, sliced
Salt and black pepper, to taste
1 teaspoon dried basil
½ teaspoon dried thyme
½ teaspoon dried sage
1 (20-ounce) package frozen peas
2½ pounds chicken, cut in pieces
5½ cups water
¾ cup rice, uncooked

Place all ingredients except rice into a slow cooker in order listed. Cover and cook 1 hour on high; reduce to low and cook for an additional 8 to 9 hours. One hour before serving, remove chicken and cool slightly. Remove meat from bones and return to slow cooker. Add rice. Cover and cook an additional hour on high. Makes 8 servings.

Hot and Sour Soup

3 (14-ounce) cans low-sodium chicken broth
8 ounces boneless, skinless chicken breasts, cut into ¼-inch-thick strips
1 cup shredded carrots
1 cup thinly sliced mushrooms
½ cup julienned bamboo shoots
3 tablespoons rice vinegar
½ to ¾ teaspoon white pepper
¼ to ½ teaspoon hot pepper sauce
2 tablespoons cornstarch
2 tablespoons low-sodium soy sauce
2 medium green onions, sliced
1 egg, slightly beaten

Combine chicken broth, chicken, carrots, mushrooms, bamboo shoots, vinegar, pepper, and hot pepper sauce in large saucepan. Bring to a boil over medium-high heat; reduce heat to low. Cover and simmer for about 5 minutes, or until chicken is no longer pink in center. Stir together cornstarch and soy sauce in small bowl until smooth. Add to chicken broth mixture. Cook and stir until mixture comes to a boil. Stir in green onions and egg. Cook for about 1 minute, stirring in one direction, until egg is cooked. Makes 4 servings.

Mexican Chicken Soup

2 pounds boneless, skinless chicken breasts, cut into cubes
3 cups chicken stock or broth
1 (15-ounce) can black soybeans
1 cup chopped tomatoes
1 cup chopped scallions, divided
¼ cup chopped jalapeños
2 garlic cloves, crushed
½ teaspoon ground cumin
½ teaspoon diced Mexican oregano
2 tablespoons lime juice
1 cup shredded Cheddar cheese
½ cup sour cream

Mix chicken, broth, soybeans, tomatoes, ¾ cup scallions (including all of the white parts), jalapeños, garlic, cumin, and oregano in a slow cooker. Cover and cook on high for 1 hour and then on low for at least 5 hours. Add lime juice and mix well. Place in individual bowls, and top evenly with cheese, sour cream, and reserved scallions. Makes 6 servings.

Old-Fashioned Chicken Soup

2 carrots, diced
1 medium onion, chopped
2 celery stalks, chopped
6 cups low-sodium chicken broth
6 ounces uncooked dried noodles
2 boneless, skinless chicken breasts, cooked and cubed
¼ teaspoon salt

Put carrots, onion, celery, and broth into a Dutch oven. Heat to boiling. Cover and boil gently about 10 minutes. Add noodles. Cook until the noodles are tender. Add chicken and salt. Heat to boiling. Makes 4 servings.

Peanut Soup with Chicken

8 Roma tomatoes, halved and seeded
4 tablespoons peanut oil, divided
Salt and black pepper, to taste
1 tablespoon curry powder
1 cup sliced onions
1½ teaspoons minced garlic
¼ teaspoon cayenne pepper
1 quart chicken broth
¾ pound sweet potatoes, roasted and skin removed
½ cup smooth peanut butter
1 cup unsweetened coconut milk
1¾ teaspoons salt
½ teaspoon white pepper
1½ pounds boneless, skinless chicken breast, cut into 1-inch cubes
2 tablespoons chopped fresh cilantro leaves
2 tablespoons chopped roasted peanuts

Place tomatoes in a small mixing bowl and coat with 1 tablespoon of peanut oil. Lay tomatoes on a baking sheet, skin side up, and season with salt and pepper. Roast tomatoes at 400° until skins are caramelized and wilted, about 25 to 30 minutes. Let cool, discard skins, and set aside until ready to use.

Set a stockpot over a medium-high heat, and add 2 tablespoons of peanut oil. Add curry powder to pot, and toast for about 30 to 45 seconds, stirring constantly. Add onions and sauté for 3 to 4 minutes. Add minced garlic and cook, stirring, for 30 seconds. Add cayenne pepper and chicken broth, and bring to a boil. Reduce the heat to a simmer. Add roasted sweet potatoes and tomatoes to the soup. Add the peanut butter and coconut milk and stir to blend. Let simmer for 10 minutes, and blend with an immersion blender or in batches in a blender until smooth. Season with ¾ teaspoon salt and, if necessary, more pepper.

Season the chicken pieces with the remaining teaspoon of salt and the white pepper, and sear in a hot sauté pan with the remaining 1 tablespoon of peanut oil for 5 minutes. Add the seared chicken to the pot. Cook until the chicken is tender, about 10 to 15 minutes.

To serve, ladle the soup into bowls, and garnish with cilantro and chopped peanuts. Makes 6 servings.

Rustic Stew

2 to 3 pounds boneless, skinless chicken breasts
1 tablespoon butter
2 teaspoons garlic, minced
2 (10¾-ounce) cans chicken broth
1¼ pounds small red potatoes, halved
1 cup baby carrots
1 cup sliced celery
½ cup small boiling onions
2 teaspoons dried thyme
1 cup portobello mushrooms, halved

Brown chicken in a skillet with garlic and butter. Pour broth in a slow cooker. Add potatoes, carrots, celery, onion, thyme, and mushrooms. Place chicken on top. Cover and cook on low for 7 to 9 hours. Makes 8 servings.

Senegalese Soup

2 egg yolks, beaten
1 cup half-and-half
1 teaspoon curry powder
Dash cayenne pepper
Salt to taste
3 cups hot chicken broth
1 cup cooked and chopped chicken
Juice and zest of 1 lemon
¼ cup chopped fresh parsley

Combine beaten egg yolks, half-and-half, curry powder, cayenne pepper, and salt in a saucepan; mix well. Slowly add hot chicken broth, stirring constantly. Cook and stir over low heat until soup thickens. Add chicken, lemon juice, lemon zest, and parsley. Cook until just heated through. Makes 4 servings.

Slow Cooker Chicken Soup

1 tablespoon olive oil
1 tablespoon butter
1 pound boneless, skinless chicken thighs, chopped
2 stalks celery, with leaves, sliced
2 large carrots, sliced
1 onion, chopped
1 (14-ounce) can diced tomatoes, undrained
1 (14-ounce) can chicken broth
1 teaspoon dried thyme
½ teaspoon salt
⅛ teaspoon black pepper
1 (9-ounce) package frozen green peas
1 cup refrigerated egg noodles

Heat olive oil and butter in a skillet over medium heat. Add chicken and cook, stirring frequently, for 5 minutes. Place chicken and remaining ingredients, except peas and noodles, in a slow cooker and stir to mix. Cover and cook on low for 6½ to 7 hours, or until chicken is thoroughly cooked. Stir in peas and noodles, and cook 10 minutes longer, until noodles are tender and soup is thoroughly heated. Makes 8 servings.

Slow Cooker Chicken Stew

2 pounds boneless, skinless chicken breasts, cut into 1-inch cubes
3 medium onions, peeled and quartered
2 large carrots, peeled, cut into 1-inch-thick slices
2 potatoes, peeled, cut into 1-inch cubes
2 (14-ounce) cans chicken broth
1 teaspoon celery seed
1 teaspoon dried thyme
½ teaspoon black pepper
8 ounces fresh mushrooms, halved
1 cup frozen corn
1 cup frozen peas

In a slow cooker, combine the chicken, onions, carrots, potatoes, and broth. Stir in the celery seeds, thyme, pepper, mushrooms, and corn. Cover and cook on low until the chicken is done and the vegetables are tender, about 7 to 9 hours, or on high for 4 to 6 hours. Stir in peas and cook until done, about 15 to 30 minutes. Makes 8 servings.

Spinach Chicken Noodle Soup

4 (14-ounce) cans of chicken broth
1 cup chopped onion
1 cup sliced carrot
2 (10-ounce) cans cream of chicken soup
1 (10-ounce) package frozen chopped spinach, thawed
4 cups boneless, skinless chicken, cooked and chopped
2 cups uncooked egg noodles
½ teaspoon salt
½ teaspoon black pepper

Combine broth, onion, and carrot in a large pot. Bring to a boil, cover, reduce heat, and simmer for 15 minutes. Add cream of chicken soup and remaining ingredients. Bring to a boil, reduce heat, and simmer uncovered for another 15 minutes. Makes 8 servings.

Sweet and Sour Chicken Stew

1 pound boneless, skinless chicken breasts, cut into 1-inch pieces
1 (9-ounce) package baby carrots
1 onion, chopped
1 (14-ounce) can condensed chicken broth
1½ cups water
1 tablespoon fresh ginger, finely chopped
1 (10-ounce) jar sweet and sour simmer sauce
1 (8-ounce) can pineapple chunks, drained, juice reserved
2 tablespoons cornstarch
1 red bell pepper, chopped
1 yellow bell pepper, chopped
1 cup dried thin egg noodles

Combine chicken, carrots, onion, chicken broth, water, ginger, and sweet and sour sauce in a slow cooker. Cover and cook on low for 7 to 8 hours, until vegetables are tender and chicken is thoroughly cooked.

Mix reserved pineapple juice with cornstarch until smooth, and stir into chicken mixture, mixing well. Stir in pineapple, bell peppers, and egg noodles. Cover and cook on high for 25 to 35 minutes, or until pasta is tender and vegetables are heated through. Makes 6 to 8 servings.

Thai Chicken and Coconut Milk Soup

Juice of 1 lime
¼ pound boneless, skinless chicken breast, cut into small chunks
1 (12-ounce) can coconut milk
1 (4-inch) piece of lemon grass, cut into very thin, ⅟₁₆-inch slices on the diagonal
1 teaspoon grated lime zest
3 to 4 slices fresh ginger
Hot chile peppers, cut into thin circles
Chopped fresh cilantro

Pour lime juice over chicken, and marinate for 15 to 30 minutes. Meanwhile, in a medium saucepan, combine coconut milk, lemon grass, lime zest, ginger, and chile peppers. Bring to a simmer. Add the chicken and stir. Reduce heat and simmer for 12 to 15 minutes, or until the chicken is done. Garnish with cilantro. Makes 2 servings.

White Chicken Chili

1 teaspoon vegetable oil
2 garlic cloves, minced
2 medium onions, chopped
2 (15-ounce) cans great northern beans
3 cups chicken broth
4 cups cooked, shredded chicken
2 (4-ounce) cans chopped green chiles
2 teaspoons ground cumin
1½ teaspoons dried oregano
¼ teaspoon ground cloves
¼ teaspoon cayenne pepper
Grated Cheddar or Monterey Jack cheese
Sour cream

In oil over medium-high heat, sauté garlic and onion until soft. Add beans and broth to mixture. Add chicken, chiles, and spices. Cook on low for 30 to 40 minutes. Serve with cheese and sour cream for topping. Makes 4 servings.

SANDWICHES

Asian Chicken Sandwiches

1 (5-ounce) can chicken
¼ cup red bell pepper, cut into strips
¼ cup sliced green onion
¼ cup sour cream
½ teaspoon honey
½ teaspoon sesame oil
⅛ teaspoon crushed red pepper
4 slices bread
½ cup bean sprouts

In a large bowl, combine all ingredients except bread and sprouts. Spoon mixture onto bread and top with sprouts. Makes 2 servings.

Bacon Jack Chicken Sandwiches

2 teaspoons poultry seasoning
4 boneless, skinless chicken breasts
8 slices bacon, cooked and drained
4 slices pepper Jack cheese
4 hamburger buns, split
4 lettuce leaves
4 slices tomato
½ cup thinly sliced onions
12 slices dill pickle

Rub the poultry seasoning onto the chicken pieces, and grill on medium heat for about 6 minutes per side, or until no longer pink in the center. Top each piece of chicken with 2 slices of bacon and 1 slice cheese. Grill for 2 to 3 more minutes to melt the cheese. Place each piece of chicken on a bun, and top with lettuce, tomato, onion, and pickle slices before serving with your favorite condiments. Makes 4 servings.

Barbecue Chicken Burgers

1 tablespoon butter, cut into pieces
1 small red onion, ½ finely chopped, ½ thinly sliced
2 garlic cloves, finely chopped
2 tablespoons tomato paste
1 teaspoon sugar
1 tablespoon Worcestershire sauce
1 tablespoon hot pepper sauce
1¼ pounds ground chicken
1 tablespoon poultry seasoning
1 tablespoon extra-virgin olive oil
4 hamburger buns, split
2 cups prepared coleslaw, divided

In a small skillet over medium heat, melt butter. Add chopped onions, garlic, and tomato paste and cook for 5 minutes. Sprinkle in sugar and remove from heat. Transfer mixture to a bowl, and let cool for 5 minutes. Add Worcestershire and hot sauce, and stir to combine. Add chicken and seasoning, and mix well. Form 4 patties. Heat extra-virgin olive oil in a nonstick skillet over medium-high heat. Cook patties 6 minutes on each side. Serve each burger on a bun topped with ½ cup coleslaw. Makes 4 servings.

Barbecue Chicken Sandwiches

1 cup barbecue sauce
1½ cups cooked, shredded chicken
4 hamburger buns, split

Pour barbecue sauce into a saucepan, and place over medium heat until heated through, 2 to 3 minutes. Stir in chicken. Cover and simmer until chicken is hot, about 5 minutes. Fill hamburger buns with chicken mixture. Makes 4 servings.

Buffalo Chicken Sandwiches

4 teaspoons butter, softened
4 hamburger buns, split
2 cups shredded cooked chicken
3 tablespoons hot pepper sauce
1 cup shredded romaine lettuce
4 tomato slices
½ cup blue cheese or ranch dressing

Spread ½ teaspoon butter on each bun half. Broil 1 minute or until toasted. Combine chicken and hot pepper sauce in a small bowl. Spread each bun bottom with 1 tablespoon dressing, top with ½ cup chicken mixture, lettuce, tomato, and another tablespoon of dressing. Makes 4 servings.

Caesar Chicken Sandwiches

3 tablespoons all-purpose flour
½ teaspoon black pepper
4 boneless, skinless chicken breasts
6 tablespoons lemon juice
4 garlic cloves, minced
4 teaspoons Worcestershire sauce
Dash hot pepper sauce
4 teaspoons grated Parmesan cheese
4 sandwich rolls
4 leaves romaine lettuce

Combine flour and pepper. Coat chicken with flour mixture and shake off excess. Spray a nonstick skillet with cooking spray and heat over a medium heat until hot. Add chicken and lightly brown on both sides. Combine lemon juice, garlic, Worcestershire, and hot pepper sauce, and pour over chicken. Cover and simmer for 7 minutes on each side or until chicken is no longer pink. Sprinkle chicken with Parmesan. Arrange lettuce on rolls, and place chicken on top. Makes 4 servings.

Caesar Club Sandwiches

4 boneless, skinless chicken breasts
Olive oil
Salt and black pepper, to taste
4 ounces thinly sliced pancetta
1 large garlic clove, chopped
2 tablespoons chopped fresh flat-leaf parsley
1½ teaspoons anchovy paste
1 teaspoons Dijon mustard
1½ tablespoons freshly squeezed lemon juice
½ cup mayonnaise
1 large ciabatta bread
2 ounces baby arugula
12 sun-dried tomatoes in oil
2 to 3 ounces shaved Parmesan

Place chicken breasts on a sheet pan skin side up. Rub with olive oil and sprinkle with salt and pepper. Roast at 350° for 20 to 25 minutes, until cooked through. Cool slightly, and slice the meat thickly. Set aside.

Meanwhile, place the pancetta on another sheet pan in a single layer. Roast for 10 to 15 minutes, until crisp. Set aside to drain on paper towels.

Place the garlic and parsley in the bowl of a food processor, and process until minced. Add the anchovy paste, mustard, lemon juice, and mayonnaise, and process again to make a smooth dressing. Cover and place in refrigerator until ready to serve.

Slice the ciabatta in half horizontally, and separate the top from the bottom. Toast the bread in the oven, cut side up, for 5 to 7 minutes; cool slightly. Spread the cut sides of each piece with the Caesar dressing. Place half the arugula on the bottom piece of bread, and then layer in order: the sun-dried tomatoes, shaved Parmesan, crispy pancetta, and sliced chicken. Sprinkle with salt and pepper, and finish with another layer of arugula. Place the top slice of ciabatta on top and cut into quarters. Serve at room temperature. Makes 4 servings.

Chicken and Artichoke Parmesan Hoagies

4 (12-inch) loaves Italian bread, halved lengthwise
1 (32-ounce) jar tomato sauce
16 fried chicken fingers
1 (12-ounce) jar marinated artichokes, drained
1 pound thinly sliced fresh mozzarella
½ cup finely grated Parmesan cheese

Arrange bottom halves of bread loaves on a large baking sheet and tops on another large baking sheet, all with cut sides up. Spread ¼ cup tomato sauce on each top and bottom. Place 4 chicken fingers on each loaf. Top each open-faced sandwich with ¼ cup tomato sauce, ¼ of the artichokes, ¼ of the mozzarella, and 1 tablespoon Parmesan.

Bake open-faced sandwiches in lower third of oven at 400° until cheese melts, about 3 minutes. When cheese begins to melt, put tops of loaves in upper third of oven and bake until edges are golden, 3 to 4 minutes. Put tops on bottoms to make sandwiches, then slice each in half. Makes 8 servings.

Chicken and Sausage Sandwiches with Sautéed Bell Peppers

4 teaspoons olive oil
4 red bell peppers, seeded and sliced
1 large yellow onion, thinly sliced
4 boneless, skinless chicken breasts, cooked and sliced into thin strips
1 cup diced chorizo or andouille sausage
2 tablespoons balsamic vinegar
Salt and black pepper, to taste
4 submarine or hoagie rolls

Heat the olive oil in a large skillet over medium-high heat. Add bell peppers and sauté 5 minutes until tender. Remove half of the peppers from skillet and set aside. Add onion and sauté 3 minutes until soft. Add sliced chicken, sausage, and balsamic vinegar. Cook 2 minutes to heat through. Season to taste with salt and black pepper. Spoon mixture on rolls and top with reserved peppers. Makes 4 servings.

Chicken Cordon Bleu Burgers

2 tablespoons vegetable or olive oil, plus more for drizzling
4 slices Canadian bacon
2 pounds ground chicken breast
2 teaspoons sweet paprika
2 teaspoons poultry seasoning
1 teaspoon salt
1 teaspoon pepper
1 shallot, finely chopped
4 deli slices Swiss cheese
⅔ cup mayonnaise
3 tablespoons Dijon mustard
2 tablespoons freshly chopped tarragon leaves
4 kaiser rolls, split and toasted
8 leaves leaf lettuce
1 tomato, thinly sliced

Add 2 tablespoons oil to a nonstick skillet over medium heat. Cook Canadian bacon until edges caramelize, 1 to 2 minutes on each side. Remove to a piece of foil. Fold foil over loosely to keep warm.

Combine chicken, paprika, poultry seasoning, salt, pepper, and shallot. Make 4 large patties, ¾- to 1-inch thick. Place in skillet drizzle with oil, and cook 5 minutes on each side, until chicken is cooked through. Top patties with Canadian bacon and Swiss cheese (fold cheese to fit burger). Cover loosely with tin foil. Turn off pan and let cheese melt, 2 minutes.

Combine mayonnaise, mustard, and tarragon. Slather rolls with sauce, place burgers on rolls, and top with lettuce and tomato. Makes 4 servings.

Chicken Pitas

2 (5-ounce) cans chicken
½ cup ranch salad dressing
4 pita breads, cut in half
8 lettuce leaves
8 tomato slices

In a bowl, combine chicken and dressing. Divide mixture evenly among pita halves. Top with lettuce and tomato. Makes 8 servings.

Chicken Tea Sandwiches

2 cups cooked and cubed chicken
1 medium unpeeled red apple, chopped
¾ cup dried cranberries
½ cup thinly sliced celery
¼ cup chopped pecans
2 tablespoons thinly sliced green onions
¾ cup mayonnaise or salad dressing
2 teaspoons lime juice
12 slices bread
Lettuce Leaves

In a bowl, combine the first six ingredients. Combine mayonnaise and lime juice; add to chicken mixture and stir to coat. Cover and refrigerate until ready to serve. Cut crusts off bread. Top with lettuce and chicken salad. Makes 6 servings.

Cream Cheese Chicken Sandwiches

4 ounces cream cheese, softened
4 teaspoons dried dill weed, divided
4 tablespoons minced garlic, divided
2 tablespoons butter, softened
2 boneless, skinless chicken breasts
2 lettuce leaves
1 small tomato, diced
4 (1-inch thick) slices French bread

In a medium bowl, mix together cream cheese, 2 teaspoons dill, and 2 tablespoons garlic. Set aside. Melt about half of the butter in a skillet over medium heat. Season chicken breasts with remaining garlic and dill. Cook for about 8 minutes per side, or until meat is firm and juices run clear. Remove from pan, and set aside. Spread remaining butter onto one side of the slices of bread, and toast in the skillet until golden. Spread cream cheese onto the other sides of the bread, and make sandwiches with chicken breasts, lettuce, and tomato. Makes 2 servings.

Curried Chicken Salad Sandwiches

3 tablespoons extra-virgin olive oil
4 boneless, skinless chicken breasts
Salt and black pepper, to taste
½ cup mayonnaise
1 teaspoon curry powder
Juice of half a lemon
¼ cup chopped, blanched almonds, toasted
¼ cup raisins
Fresh basil leaves, torn
8 slices dense white bread

Heat oil in a large ovenproof skillet over medium-high heat until smoking. Sprinkle chicken breasts on both sides with salt and pepper. Put in pan in a single layer, and brown 2 minutes on each side. Put skillet in oven and roast at 400° until chicken is just cooked through, about 15 minutes. Remove from oven and cool. Chop cooled chicken and put it into a large bowl. Add the rest of the salad ingredients, and toss. Season with salt and pepper. Spread on bread slices to make sandwiches. Makes 4 servings.

Gourmet Chicken Sandwiches

Black pepper, to taste
4 boneless, skinless chicken breasts, pounded to ¼-inch thickness
1 tablespoon olive oil
1 teaspoon minced garlic
2 tablespoons mayonnaise
2 teaspoons Dijon mustard
1 teaspoon chopped fresh rosemary
8 slices garlic and rosemary focaccia bread

Sprinkle pepper on one side of each chicken cutlet. Heat oil in a large skillet; brown garlic in oil, then add chicken, pepper-side down. Sauté chicken until cooked through and juices run clear, about 12 to 15 minutes. In a small bowl, combine the mayonnaise, mustard, and rosemary. Mix together and spread on 4 slices focaccia bread. Place 1 chicken cutlet on each of these slices, and top with another bread slice. Makes 4 servings.

Grilled Chicken Sandwiches

1 garlic clove, minced
¼ cup lemon juice
1 tablespoon olive oil
1 teaspoon oregano
4 boneless, skinless chicken breasts
4 sourdough sandwich rolls, halved
4 slices red onion
¼ cup mayonnaise
4 slices tomato
4 lettuce leaves

Combine first 4 ingredients in a shallow glass dish. Add chicken breasts and turn to coat. Marinate 1 hour. Grill 4 to 5 minutes per side, or until chicken is done. Grill sandwich roll halves and red onion slices for 1 minute until bread is golden. Spread mayonnaise on both sides of rolls. Place chicken on rolls and top with sliced tomato, lettuce, and onion. Makes 4 servings.

Italian Chicken Wraps

4 boneless, skinless chicken breasts
1 cup Italian Dressing
1 teaspoon Italian seasoning
8 tortillas
⅓ cup shredded mozzarella cheese
½ cup arugula
Dijon mustard

Marinate chicken in dressing and seasoning for at least 1 hour. Grill chicken over medium heat for 5 to 7 minutes on each side. Cut into wide strips. Place a few chicken strips on each tortilla, and top with a sprinkling of cheese, a few arugula leaves, and a little mustard. Roll up. Makes 8 servings.

Pesto Chicken Sandwiches

4 boneless, skinless chicken breasts
Salt and pepper, to taste
¼ cup pesto sauce
4 sandwich buns
4 tomato slices
¼ cup freshly grated Parmesan cheese

Season chicken with salt and pepper, and grill over medium heat for 5 to 7 minutes on each side. Spread about 4 teaspoons pesto onto each bun, and top with chicken, tomato, and Parmesan cheese. Makes 4 servings.

Smoky Orange Barbecue Chicken Sandwiches

1 tablespoon olive or vegetable oil, plus some for drizzling
1 small onion, chopped
3 chipotle peppers in adobo sauce
½ cup ketchup
¼ cup orange juice concentrate
1 orange, zested and cut into wedges, for garnish
1 cup chicken broth
4 boneless, skinless chicken breasts
Poultry seasoning
4 crusty rolls, split, toasted, and buttered
Romaine lettuce
Sliced red onions

Heat a small saucepan over moderate heat. Add 1 tablespoon oil and sauté onion for 3 to 5 minutes, or until soft. Combine chipotle peppers in adobo, ketchup, orange juice concentrate, orange zest, and chicken broth in a blender. Blend on high until sauce is smooth. Pour sauce into saucepan with onion and heat till bubbly. Reserve half of sauce.

Coat chicken lightly with a drizzle of oil and sprinkle of seasoning. Grill 5 to 6 minutes on the first side; turn. Baste chicken liberally with sauce. Turn chicken after 4 minutes, coat with sauce again, and cook another 2 to 3 minutes.

To serve sandwiches, slice grilled chicken on an angle and fan out 1 breast on each bun bottom. Spoon remaining sauce over sliced chicken. Serve open faced with lettuce and red onion on the side. Makes 4 servings.

Teriyaki Chicken Sandwiches

½ cup vegetable oil
¼ cup soy sauce
3 tablespoons honey
2 tablespoons white vinegar
1 tablespoon minced garlic
4 boneless, skinless chicken breasts
4 croissants
1 cup finely shredded lettuce
8 tomato slices
4 green bell pepper rings

Combine vegetable oil, soy sauce, honey, vinegar, ginger, and garlic. Reserve ¼ cup and pour remaining sauce into a large resealable plastic bag. Add chicken and marinate in the refrigerator for at least 2 hours or up to 8 hours. Remove chicken and grill over medium heat for 5 to 7 minutes on each side. On the bottom half of each croissant, layer lettuce, tomato, chicken, and bell pepper. Drizzle with reserved sauce. Makes 4 servings.

Waldorf Chicken Salad Sandwiches

4 kaiser rolls, cut in half
1 cup chicken salad
12 very thin apple slices
4 slices Cheddar cheese

Layer bottom half of each roll with ¼ cup salad, 3 apple slices, and 1 cheese slice. Top with remaining halves. Makes 4 servings.

MAIN COURSES

15-Minute Chicken, Rice, and Broccoli Dinner

1 tablespoon oil
4 boneless, skinless chicken breasts
1 (10¾-ounce) can low-sodium cream of chicken soup
1½ cups water
2 cups quick-cooking rice
2 cups fresh broccoli florets

Heat oil in large nonstick skillet on medium-high heat. Add chicken; cook 4 minutes on each side or until cooked through. Remove from skillet. Add soup and water to skillet. Bring to boil. Stir in rice and broccoli. Top with chicken; cover. Cook on low heat for 5 minutes. Makes 4 servings.

Almond Chicken

¼ cup butter
¼ cup flour
2 cups chicken broth
2 eggs, beaten
1 cup mayonnaise
4 cups cooked and chopped chicken
1 cup chow mein noodles
½ cup slivered almonds

Melt butter in medium saucepan; add flour and cook for 4 minutes. Gradually add chicken broth, cooking and stirring until smooth and bubbly. Add remaining ingredients and pour into a greased 2-quart casserole. Bake at 350° for about 45 minutes. Makes 4 servings.

Aloha Chicken

⅓ cup steak sauce
2 tablespoons honey
1 (8-ounce) can pineapple chunks, drained, 2 tablespoons juice reserved
1 medium green bell pepper, chopped
4 boneless, skinless chicken breasts

Mix steak sauce with honey and reserved pineapple juice. Place green peppers in the bottom of a slow cooker. Add chicken breasts on top. Pour honey mixture over the chicken breasts. Cover and cook on low for 4 to 6 hours. Add pineapple chunks and cook an additional 30 to 60 minutes. Makes 4 servings.

Apricot Chicken

4 boneless, skinless chicken breasts
1 tablespoon freshly grated ginger
½ cup apricot preserves
⅓ cup Italian salad dressing

Combine all ingredients in a large plastic bag. Shake bag to mix; refrigerate at least 2 hours and up to 24 hours. When ready to cook, place chicken in a slow cooker; reserve marinade. Cover and cook on low for 6 to 8 hours, until chicken is thoroughly cooked, basting occasionally with marinade. Discard remaining marinade. Makes 4 servings.

Asian Chicken Stir-Fry

2 tablespoons olive oil
1 teaspoon sesame oil
3 boneless chicken breasts, cut into strips
1 onion, chopped
1 red bell pepper, chopped
1 carrot, chopped
2 cups fresh broccoli, chopped
2 tablespoons soy sauce
1 (8-ounce) can pineapple chunks
1 tablespoon cornstarch
¼ cup water
2 cups rice, cooked and hot

Heat olive oil and sesame oil in large skillet; add chicken and cook 2 minutes. Add onion, red bell pepper, carrot, broccoli, and soy sauce; cook and stir several minutes. Add pineapple and cook about 10 minutes more. Combine cornstarch and water; add to chicken mixture and cook until thickened. Serve over rice. Makes 4 to 6 servings.

Asian-Spiced Chicken and Beans

1 pound canned navy beans, drained and rinsed
1 pound canned red beans, drained and rinsed
1 pound boneless, skinless chicken breasts, cut into ½-inch cubes
3 carrots, diagonally sliced
2½ teaspoons minced garlic
2½ teaspoons minced fresh ginger root, or 1½ teaspoons ground ginger
1¾ cups low-sodium chicken broth, divided
2 tablespoons cornstarch
½ teaspoon red pepper flakes
2½ tablespoons soy sauce
4 cups cooked rice

Place beans, chicken, carrots, garlic, ginger, and 1¼ cups chicken broth in a slow cooker; stir well. Cover and cook on low until ingredients are tender, about 5 hours. Turn slow cooker to high. Stir in combined cornstarch and remaining chicken broth; stir in red pepper. Cover and cook until thickened, about 30 minutes. Stir in soy sauce. Serve over rice. Makes 4 servings.

Baked Chicken and Stuffing

1 (8-ounce) bag herb-seasoned stuffing mix, prepared according to
   package directions
6 boneless, skinless chicken breasts
1 (10¾-ounce) can cream of chicken soup
¾ cup milk

Sprinkle stuffing in bottom of a greased baking dish; place chicken breasts on top. Combine soup and milk, and pour over chicken. Bake at 400° for about 30 minutes. Makes 6 servings.

Baked Chicken Breasts

1½ cups plain yogurt or sour cream
¼ cup lemon juice
½ teaspoon Worcestershire sauce
½ teaspoon celery seed
½ teaspoon sweet paprika
1 garlic clove, minced
½ teaspoon salt (optional)
¼ teaspoon black pepper
8 boneless, skinless chicken breasts
2 cups fine dry breadcrumbs

In a large bowl, combine first 8 ingredients. Place chicken in mixture, and turn to coat. Cover and marinate overnight in the refrigerator. Remove chicken from marinade; coat each piece with crumbs. Arrange on a lightly greased shallow baking pan. Bake uncovered at 350° for 45 minutes, or until juices run clear. Makes 8 servings.

Baked Chicken Parmesan

4 boneless, skinless chicken breasts (about 4 ounces each)
1 large egg
1 tablespoon water
2 teaspoons olive oil
⅓ cup finely crushed low-sodium whole grain crackers
⅓ cup shredded Parmesan cheese
2 tablespoons minced fresh parsley
½ teaspoon ground oregano
¼ teaspoon black pepper

Place each breast with the smooth side up between 2 pieces of plastic wrap. Using a tortilla press, the smooth side of a meat mallet, or a rolling pin, lightly flatten to a thickness of ¼ inch, being careful not to tear the meat. In a shallow dish or pie pan, whisk together the egg, water, and oil.

In another shallow dish or pie pan, stir together the remaining ingredients. Place the dishes side by side. Lightly spray a baking pan with vegetable oil spray. Set beside the dishes. Dip chicken into egg mixture, and turn to coat. Roll each piece in the crumb mixture, shaking off any excess. Arrange chicken in a single layer on baking sheet. Lightly spray chicken with vegetable oil spray. Bake at 400° uncovered for 15 to 18 minutes, or until chicken is no longer pink in the center and the top coating is golden brown. Makes 4 servings.

Barbecue Chicken

6 chicken thighs
½ cup barbecue sauce

Combine chicken and barbecue sauce in a large bowl, turning until chicken is evenly coated. Place chicken in a small roasting pan, leaving a little space between each piece. Cover with aluminum foil and bake at 375° for 15 minutes. Remove foil and bake an additional 25 to 30 minutes until done. Makes 6 servings.

Bisteeya

5 tablespoons butter, divided
1 cup chopped onions
Salt
Cayenne pepper
½ cup sliced almonds
1 tablespoon sugar
2 tablespoons all-purpose flour
½ cup fresh lemon juice
1½ cups chicken broth
2 large egg yolks
4 boneless, skinless chicken breasts, poached and shredded
1 teaspoon fresh lemon zest
6 sheets phyllo dough
8 tablespoons butter, melted
1 ground cinnamon
Powdered sugar

In a sauté pan over medium heat, melt 2 tablespoons butter. Add onions. Season with salt and cayenne, and sauté until translucent, about 2 minutes. Meanwhile, melt 1 tablespoon butter in a small sauté pan over medium heat. Add almonds and sprinkle with sugar. Sauté until golden brown, about 2 minutes. Remove from heat and set aside to cool.

Stir flour into the pan with the onions, and continue to cook for 1 minute. Stir in the lemon juice and broth, and bring to a boil. Add the egg yolks into the hot liquid and mix well, until you see curdling. Continue to cook for 3 to 4 minutes, or until the mixture thickens. Remove from heat and cool completely. Stir in chicken and lemon zest, and season with salt and cayenne.

Brush each sheet of phyllo with remaining melted butter, and stack each sheet on top of each other, butter side up. Line a 9-inch pie pan with buttered phyllo. Spoon chicken mixture into pan and spread evenly. Fold overlapping phyllo into pie, brushing with extra butter to seal completely. Brush the top with the remaining butter. Place on a baking sheet and bake at 375° until golden brown, about 30 minutes. Remove from oven and cool before slicing. Slice the pie into individual servings. Sprinkle the entire pie with the powdered sugar and cinnamon. Makes 6 servings.

Broiled Barbecue Chicken

4 boneless, skinless chicken breasts
½ teaspoon black pepper
1 cup bottled barbecue sauce, divided

Preheat oven broiler. Season all sides of each chicken breast with black pepper. Place chicken breast-side down under broiler for 10 minutes. Turn chicken over, and coat well with ¾ cup of sauce. Broil for 5 more minutes. Remove chicken from broiler, and coat with remaining ¼ cup of sauce. Makes 4 servings.

Brown Sugar Chicken

2 pounds boneless, skinless chicken breasts
1 cup brown sugar, packed
⅔ cup vinegar
¼ cup lemon-lime soda
2 tablespoons minced garlic
2 tablespoons soy sauce
1 teaspoon black pepper
Cooked rice

Place chicken pieces in a slow cooker. Combine remaining ingredients and pour over top of chicken. Cover and cook on low for 6 to 8 hours. Serve with rice. Makes 4 servings.

Buttermilk Chicken

¾ cup all-purpose flour
½ teaspoon salt
¼ teaspoon black pepper
4 chicken breasts
1½ cups buttermilk, divided
¼ cup butter
1 (10¾-ounce) can cream of mushroom soup

Combine flour, salt, and pepper. Dip chicken into ½ cup buttermilk. Roll in flour. Melt butter in a baking pan, and put chicken in pan. Bake uncovered for 30 minutes at 425°. Turn and bake 15 minutes more. Turn breasts again. Combine remaining buttermilk and cream of mushroom soup, and pour over chicken. Bake 15 minutes more. Makes 4 servings.

Buttermilk Fried Chicken Fingers

6 boneless, skinless chicken breasts, flattened and sliced into wide strips
Buttermilk
Flour
Salt and pepper
Vegetable oil

Place chicken in a large bowl and cover completely with buttermilk. Refrigerate 4 to 6 hours. Fill a pie plate or large shallow bowl with flour; season with salt and pepper. Heat two skillets with about a ½-inch of oil. While the oil is heating, coat the chicken fingers with the seasoned flour. Fry chicken in the oil until done, about 10 minutes per batch. Makes 6 servings.

Cajun Chicken

⅓ cup vegetable oil
3 tablespoons vinegar
1 teaspoon Italian seasoning
1 teaspoon garlic powder
¼ teaspoon black pepper
1 tablespoon Cajun seasoning
¼ teaspoon salt
2 pounds boneless, skinless chicken breasts

Combine oil, vinegar, Italian seasoning, garlic powder, black pepper, Cajun seasoning, and salt. Place chicken in a large resealable plastic bag, and pour in marinade. Marinate chicken for 20 minutes or up to 3 hours. Grill chicken, turning once. Makes 4 servings.

Cappellini Florentine

4 large garlic cloves, minced
2 tablespoons olive oil
1 (8-ounce) package sliced mushrooms
1 (10-ounce) package fresh spinach
1 tablespoon red pepper flakes
2 tablespoons balsamic vinegar
Salt and black pepper, to taste
Juice of ¼ lemon
1 (16-ounce) package dried angel hair pasta, cooked
4 chicken boneless, skinless breasts, cooked and shredded
4 ounces Mozzarella cheese, cut into cubes

In a large skillet, sauté garlic in oil over medium heat until it takes on a little color. Add mushrooms. Sauté 3 to 4 minutes until cooked through. Add spinach, stirring frequently until cooked down and wilted. Add red pepper, vinegar, salt, and pepper. Cook 1 to 2 minutes longer. Take the pan off heat and add lemon juice. Toss to distribute evenly. Combine pasta, spinach-mushroom mixture; chicken, and mozzarella. Makes 4 servings.

Cashew Chicken

1 pound boneless, skinless chicken breasts, cut into strips
¼ cup orange juice
4 teaspoons cornstarch, divided
1 teaspoon vegetable oil
¼ cup chopped cashews
1 (8-ounce) can sliced water chestnuts, drained
1 cup chopped green bell pepper
½ cup chopped green onions
1 tablespoon minced fresh ginger
1 cup nonfat, low-sodium chicken broth
2 tablespoons low-sodium soy sauce
1 (11-ounce) can mandarin oranges, drained
3 cups cooked brown rice

Combine chicken strips, orange juice, and 1 teaspoon cornstarch in a medium bowl; cover and chill 1 hour. Heat oil in a nonstick skillet over medium heat. Add cashews; cook, stirring constantly, for 30 seconds. Remove from skillet; set aside.

Add chicken mixture to skillet. Cook uncovered over medium-high heat for 8 minutes, or until chicken is lightly browned, stirring constantly. Add water chestnuts and next 3 ingredients; cook 5 minutes.

Combine broth, soy sauce, and remaining tablespoon cornstarch; add to chicken mixture. Bring to a boil: reduce heat and cook, stirring constantly, until thickened. Remove from heat; stir in oranges. Spoon chicken mixture over rice, and sprinkle with cashews. Serve immediately. Makes 4 servings.

Catalina Chicken

1 small jar apricot preserves or apricot or pineapple preserves
1 (1½-ounce) package onion soup mix
1 small bottle Catalina salad dressing
6 to 8 pieces of chicken

Combine the preserves, onion soup mix, and dressing. Spread over chicken. Bake on a greased baking sheet at 350° for 45 to 60 minutes. Makes 6 servings.

Cheese and Chicken Rollups

¼ cup butter
⅓ cup all-purpose flour
5 cups chicken broth
4 cups ground chicken
1 tablespoon finely chopped onion
¼ cup chopped pimento
Salt and black pepper, to taste
1 (10-count) can biscuit dough
½ cup processed cheese spread

In a large saucepan, melt the butter. Add flour and 3 cups chicken broth; stir until thickened. Add chicken, onion, and pimento. Season with salt and pepper, and cook until chicken is browned.

Spread biscuit dough out onto a floured surface. Spread evenly with cheese spread and then chicken mixture. Roll up like a jelly roll, seal edge, and cut into 12 slices. Place 1 inch apart on a greased baking sheet. Bake at 375° for about 30 minutes. Makes 8 servings.

Cheesy Chicken

6 boneless, skinless chicken breasts
1 (10¾-ounce) can cream of chicken soup
1 (10¾-ounce) can fiesta cheese soup
3 cups cooked rice or noodles

Place chicken breasts in a large slow cooker. Pour the undiluted soups over the chicken, and stir to combine. Cover and cook on low 6 to 8 hours, until chicken is tender and thoroughly cooked. Serve over rice or noodles. Makes 6 servings.

Chicken à la King

1 medium onion, thinly sliced
½ green bell pepper, chopped
2 tablespoons butter
4 ounces sliced mushrooms
1 (4-ounce) jar pimento, drained
1 tablespoon chicken bouillon granules
1 teaspoon all-purpose flour
½ cup water
2 cups cooked and chopped chicken
1 tablespoon lemon juice
½ teaspoon sugar
Salt and black pepper, to taste

Cook onions and pepper in butter over low heat until soft, being careful not to brown onions. Add mushrooms and pimento, and cook 2 minutes more. Combine bouillon granules with flour and water; stir into onion mixture. Add chicken and bring to a boil. Remove from heat, and add lemon juice, sugar, salt, and pepper. Makes 4 servings.

Chicken à la Marengo

1 whole chicken, cut into pieces
2 (1-ounce) packages spaghetti sauce mix
1 cup chicken stock
2 fresh tomatoes, quartered
4 ounces fresh mushrooms, sliced

Place chicken parts in bottom of a slow cooker. Combine dry spaghetti sauce packets with stock; pour over chicken. Cover and cook on low 6 to 7 hours. Add tomatoes and mushrooms. Cover and cook on high for 30 to 40 minutes, or until tomatoes are done. Makes 4 to 5 servings.

Chicken and Broccoli with Rice

4 cups cooked and chopped chicken
1 (16-ounce) package frozen chopped broccoli, thawed
1½ cups quick-cooking rice
1 (10¾-ounce) can cream of mushroom soup
1 (10¾-ounce) can cream of celery soup
½ cup milk
1 (1½-ounce) package onion soup mix
1 cup shredded Cheddar cheese

Combine chicken, broccoli, rice, soups, milk, and onion soup mix; pour into a greased casserole. Top with shredded cheese. Bake at 350° for about 45 minutes. Makes 6 to 8 servings.

Chicken and Dumplings

1 whole chicken, boiled and deboned
3 quarts plus ½ cup chicken broth
2 cups all-purpose flour
1 egg

Place chicken in 3 quarts boiling broth. Mix together ½ cup broth, flour, and egg. Roll thin. Cut into strips and drop in boiling broth. Shake dumplings down as added. Do not stir. Cook about 30 minutes or until tender. Makes 4 to 6 servings.

Chicken and Dumplings #2

4 boneless, skinless chicken breasts, cut into small chunks
2 (10¼-ounce) cans cream of chicken soup
¼ cup finely diced onion
2 cups water
1 chicken bouillon cube
2 (10-ounce) packages refrigerated biscuits

Combine all ingredients, except biscuits, in slow cooker. Cover and cook on low for 5 to 6 hours. Thirty minutes before serving, tear biscuit dough into 1-inch pieces. Add to slow cooker, stirring gently. Cover and cook on high for an additional 30 minutes, or until biscuits are cooked through. Makes 4 to 6 servings.

Chicken and Noodles

½ cup butter
1 onion, chopped
1 bell pepper, chopped
2 celery stalks, chopped
1 (8-ounce) package processed cheese, cubed
1 (10¾-ounce) can cream of mushroom soup
1 (4-ounce) can sliced mushrooms, drained
4 cups cooked and chopped chicken
1 cup chicken broth
1 (16-ounce) package dried egg noodles, cooked and drained
1 cup cheese crackers, crushed

Melt butter in large skillet; add onion, bell pepper, and celery. Cook until tender. Add cheese, soup, mushrooms, chicken, and chicken broth, cooking and stirring until cheese is melted and mixture is smooth. Stir in cooked noodles. Pour into a greased casserole, and top with crushed cheese crackers. Bake at 350° for about 45 minutes. Makes 4 servings.

Chicken and Shrimp

1 (12-ounce) package boneless, skinless chicken thighs
1 large onion, chopped
3 garlic cloves, minced
1 (14½-ounce) can Italian-style diced tomatoes
2 tablespoons tomato paste
½ cup chicken broth
2 tablespoons lemon juice
2 bay leaves
½ teaspoon salt
¼ teaspoon red pepper flakes
½ pound frozen peeled shrimp, thawed and drained
½ pound frozen artichoke hearts, thawed and coarsely chopped
2 cups dried pasta, cooked
½ cup crumbled feta cheese

Cut chicken thighs into quarters. Put onion and garlic in a slow cooker. Top with the chicken pieces. In a bowl, combine the undrained tomatoes, tomato paste, chicken broth, lemon juice, bay leaves, salt, and red pepper. Pour over all. Cover; cook on low for 6 to 7 hours. Turn to high. Remove bay leaves. Stir in shrimp and artichoke hearts. Cover; cook for 5 minutes more. Serve over pasta. Sprinkle with feta cheese. Makes 4 servings.

Chicken and Wild Rice

1 (10¾-ounce) can cream of celery soup
1 (10¾-ounce) can cream of chicken soup
1 cup chicken broth
1 (1½-ounce) package dry onion soup mix
1 (6-ounce) package quick-cooking wild rice mix
6 boneless, skinless chicken breasts

Combine soups, broth, soup mix, and wild rice mix; pour into a greased casserole. Lay chicken breasts over rice mixture. Cover tightly. Bake at 350° for about 1 hour. Makes 6 servings.

Chicken and Yellow Rice

2 pounds chicken pieces, on the bone
3 tablespoons olive oil
1 green bell pepper, chopped
1 onion, chopped
1 garlic clove, chopped
4 tomatoes, chopped
2 cups chicken broth
1 bay leaf
2 cups rice
Dash saffron

Brown chicken in olive oil in a large pot. Remove chicken and cover to keep warm. Add bell pepper, onion, garlic, tomatoes, broth, and bay leaf to the pot. Bring to a boil, then add chicken, rice, and saffron. Cover and cook until rice is done, about 20 to 25 minutes. Makes 8 servings.

Chicken Biscuit Pie

4 cups cooked and chopped chicken
2 cups chicken broth
4 hard-boiled eggs, peeled and chopped
1 (10¾-ounce) can cream of chicken soup
1 (20-ounce) package frozen mixed vegetables, thawed
1 (10-count) can refrigerated biscuit dough

Combine chicken, broth, eggs, soup, and vegetables; pour into a greased baking dish. Top with biscuit dough. Bake at 350° for about 30 minutes. Makes about 4 servings.

Chicken Breasts with Lemon Sauce

4 boneless, skinless chicken breasts
Garlic salt to taste
Black pepper, to taste
1 cup nonfat low-sodium chicken broth
1½ tablespoons fresh lemon juice
½ teaspoon grated lemon zest
¼ cup nonfat grated Parmesan cheese
⅓ cup nonfat sour cream
1 tablespoon all-purpose flour

Season chicken breasts with garlic salt and black pepper. Spray skillet with nonstick cooking spray. Add chicken breasts, brown, and cook over medium heat until done, about 4 to 5 minutes on each side. In medium saucepan, combine chicken broth, lemon juice, lemon zest, cheese, and sour cream. Use flour and a small amount of broth to make a thin paste. Stir paste back into sauce, and stir over medium heat until thickened. Pour over cooked chicken breasts. Makes 4 servings.

Chicken Breasts with New Potatoes

¼ **cup butter**
4 to 6 large chicken breasts, on the bone
1 onion, sliced
1 garlic clove, minced
2 tablespoons all-purpose flour
½ **teaspoon salt**
¼ **teaspoon black pepper**
1 chicken bouillon cube
1 cup hot water
8 new potatoes, boiled

Melt butter in a large skillet, and sauté chicken on both sides until brown. Add onion and garlic, and cook about 5 minutes. In a small bowl, combine flour, salt, and pepper. Dissolve bouillon cube in hot water, and slowly pour over browned chicken. Cover and cook on low heat for about 25 minutes, or until chicken is tender. Add new potatoes and heat through. Makes 4 to 6 servings.

Chicken Cacciatore

1 pound boneless, skinless chicken breast strips
1 onion, chopped
1 red bell pepper, chopped
1 teaspoon minced garlic
2 tablespoons olive oil
2 (14-ounce) cans diced tomatoes
1 (8-ounce) can tomato sauce
1 teaspoon Italian seasoning
Salt and black pepper, to taste
2 cups cooked rice

Brown chicken, onion, bell pepper, and garlic in oil. Add tomatoes, tomato sauce, Italian seasoning, salt, and pepper. Bring to a boil, reduce heat, cover, and simmer until chicken is thoroughly cooked. Serve over rice. Makes 4 servings.

Chicken Casserole with Rice

1 (3-pound) chicken, cut into pieces
Salt and pepper, to taste
6 slices bacon
2 cups quick-cooking rice
1 (10¾-ounce) can cream of mushroom soup
2 cups milk

Season chicken with salt and pepper. Arrange bacon in baking dish. Sprinkle rice over bacon. Arrange chicken over rice. Pour mixture of soup and milk over top. Bake at 350° for 90 minutes. Makes 6 servings.

Chicken Casserole with Vegetables

1½ pounds boneless, skinless chicken breasts
6 carrots, sliced
1 (8-ounce) can green beans
2 (10¾-ounce) cans cream of mushroom soup
2 tablespoons mayonnaise
½ cup shredded Cheddar cheese

Place chicken in bottom of a slow cooker. Mix carrots, green beans, mushroom soup, and mayonnaise. Pour over chicken. Cover and cook for 8 to 10 hours on low. Sprinkle with Cheddar cheese before serving. Makes 6 to 8 servings.

Chicken Cordon Bleu

6 boneless, skinless chicken breasts
6 pieces Swiss cheese
6 slices ham
1 (10¾-ounce) can condensed cream of mushroom soup with roasted garlic
3 tablespoons water
¼ teaspoon black pepper

Flatten each chicken breast with a wooden mallet or rolling pin. Place a piece of cheese and a slice of ham in the center of each. Fold up and secure with toothpicks. Place in a slow cooker. Combine remaining ingredients and pour over chicken bundles, making sure pieces are fully covered. Cover and cook on low for 6 to 7 hours. Makes 6 servings.

Chicken Croquettes

1½ cups chicken broth
2½ cups dry breadcrumbs, divided
1 medium onion, finely chopped
2 eggs, beaten
2 tablespoons Worcestershire sauce
1 tablespoon lemon juice
1 teaspoon sugar
Salt and black pepper, to taste
2 cups chicken, cooked and finely chopped

Combine chicken broth, 1½ cups breadcrumbs, onion, eggs, Worcestershire sauce, lemon juice, sugar, salt, and pepper; mix well. Fold in chicken. Form into small patties, about 2 inches thick, and roll in remaining breadcrumbs. Bake at 375° for about 20 minutes until golden. Makes 4 servings.

Chicken Curry

1 pound boneless, skinless chicken breast, cut into cubes
½ cup chopped onion
2 garlic cloves, minced
1 medium head cauliflower, cut into florets
2 medium potatoes, peeled and cubed
2 large carrots, sliced
1½ cups chicken broth
¾ teaspoon ground turmeric
¼ teaspoon dry mustard
¼ teaspoon ground cumin
¼ teaspoon ground coriander
1 tablespoon flour
2 tablespoons cold water
1 large tomato, chopped
2 tablespoons finely chopped parsley
1 to 2 tablespoons lemon juice
Salt and cayenne pepper, to taste

Coat a large saucepan with cooking spray, and place over medium heat. Sauté chicken, onion, and garlic until chicken is browned, 5 to 6 minutes. Add cauliflower, potatoes, carrots, broth, and herbs to saucepan; heat to boiling. Reduce heat and simmer, covered, until chicken and vegetables are tender, 10 to 15 minutes.

Heat mixture to boiling. Mix flour and water; stir into boiling mixture. Cook, stirring constantly, until thickened. Stir in tomato, parsley, and lemon juice; simmer 2 to 3 minutes longer. Season with salt and cayenne pepper. Makes 4 servings.

Chicken Cutlets with Ginger Mustard Sauce

1 pound chicken cutlets
¼ teaspoon ground ginger
Salt and black pepper to taste
1 tablespoon olive oil
¼ cup water
1½ teaspoons cornstarch
½ cup chicken broth
1 tablespoon Dijon mustard
2 teaspoons peeled and chopped fresh ginger
3 tablespoons sour cream

Season chicken with ginger, salt, and pepper; sauté in olive oil until just cooked through. Remove from pan, and cover to keep warm. Combine water and cornstarch, stirring until cornstarch is dissolved. Add cornstarch mixture, chicken broth, Dijon mustard, and fresh ginger to skillet. Cook, whisking constantly, until mixture thickens; remove from heat. Pour any chicken juices back into skillet, and add sour cream; whisk until smooth and pour over chicken cutlets. Makes 4 servings.

Chicken Dijon

8 ounces plain low-fat yogurt
¼ cup Dijon mustard
8 chicken breasts, on the bone, skin removed
½ cup soft breadcrumbs

Combine yogurt and mustard, stirring until well blended. Brush breasts evenly with yogurt mixture, and dredge in breadcrumbs. Arrange chicken in a baking dish coated with cooking spray. Cover and bake at 400° for 30 minutes. Increase temperature to 450°. Bake uncovered for 15 minutes, or until chicken is done and coating is browned. Makes 8 servings.

Chicken Dinner

1 (3-pound) whole chicken
8 large carrots, peeled, cooked, and cut into 2-inch pieces
6 potatoes, peeled and sliced
1 (1-ounce) package onion soup mix
1 teaspoon dried basil
1 cup chicken broth

Place chicken, carrots, and potatoes in a slow cooker. Combine remaining ingredients in a bowl, and pour over. Cover and cook on high about 5 hours or on low about 9 hours, until chicken leg and thigh come off easily when pulled. Makes 4 servings.

Chicken Divan

1 (10-ounce) package frozen broccoli spears, thawed and drained
2 to 3 boneless, skinless chicken breasts
1 (10¾-ounce) can cream of chicken soup
1¼ cups mayonnaise
1 teaspoon lemon juice

Place broccoli in the bottom of a slow cooker. Put chicken on top of broccoli. Mix together soup, mayonnaise, and lemon juice. Pour over chicken, mixing slightly. Cover and cook on low for 8 hours. Makes 2 to 3 servings.

Chicken Enchiladas

8 corn tortillas, stacked and wrapped in foil
1¼ cups salsa verde
½ cup sour cream
¼ cup chopped cilantro
1½ cups cooked and diced chicken breast
1½ cups shredded Swiss cheese, divided
1 (7-ounce) jar roasted red peppers, sliced
Diced tomato and sliced scallion

Warm tortillas in oven at 425°. Mix salsa, sour cream, and cilantro in a medium bowl. Spread ½ cup over bottom of a baking dish. In another bowl, combine chicken, 1 cup cheese, and roasted peppers.

Remove tortillas from oven. Spoon scant ½ cup chicken mixture down center of each tortilla. Roll up; place seam-side down in baking dish. Pour remaining salsa mixture over top. Cover with foil and bake 15 minutes until bubbly. Uncover, sprinkle with remaining cheese, and bake 10 minutes, or until cheese has melted. Makes 8 servings.

Chicken Fajitas

1 tablespoon olive oil
1 pound boneless, skinless chicken breasts, cut into strips
⅓ cup beef broth
2 tablespoons molasses
1 tablespoon lemon juice
1 tablespoon lime juice
1 teaspoon minced garlic
1 onion, sliced
1 red bell pepper, sliced
Salt and black pepper, to taste
8 (10-inch) flour tortillas

Heat olive oil in large skillet; add chicken and cook thoroughly. Remove chicken from pan. Add beef broth, molasses, lemon juice, lime juice, and garlic to skillet; bring to a boil, scraping up browned bits of chicken. Add onion, salt, and pepper; cook and stir until tender. Return chicken to skillet, and heat through. Serve with tortillas. Makes 4 servings.

Chicken Fettuccini Florentine

½ **pound fettuccini noodles**
½ **pound spinach fettuccini noodles**
1 **(10-ounce) box frozen spinach, cooked and drained**
1 **(10¾-ounce) can creamy chicken mushroom soup**
1 **soup can milk**
2 **tablespoons garlic powder**
1 **cup all-purpose flour**
Salt and black pepper, to taste
6 **boneless, skinless chicken breasts, pounded thin**
1 **tablespoon olive oil**
½ **cup grated Parmesan cheese**
1½ **cups shredded mozzarella cheese**

Cook both kinds of noodles together; drain and set aside. In a saucepan, combine spinach, chicken soup, milk, and garlic powder. Bring to a light boil; set aside.

Season flour with salt and pepper. Dredge chicken breasts in flour. Warm olive oil in a skillet over medium heat. Brown chicken breasts on both sides in oil.

Toss noodles with spinach mixture, and pour into bottom of baking dish. Sprinkle with Parmesan cheese, arrange chicken breasts on top, and sprinkle with mozzarella cheese. Bake at 350° for 20 to 30 minutes. Makes 6 servings.

Chicken Florentine

4 boneless, skinless chicken breasts
Salt and black pepper, to taste
1 cup all-purpose flour
6 tablespoons butter, divided
2 tablespoons sliced shallots
1 tablespoon minced garlic
1½ cups chicken broth
1 cup heavy cream
1 tablespoon chopped parsley
2 (10-ounce) packages frozen chopped spinach, thawed and drained

Season chicken with salt and pepper, and dredge in flour. Melt 2 tablespoons butter in a large skillet over medium heat. Brown the chicken in the butter, about 5 minutes per side. Transfer the chicken to a plate.

Melt 2 more tablespoons butter in the skillet over medium heat. Add shallots and garlic and sauté until shallots are translucent, about 1 minute. Add broth. Increase heat to medium high, and boil until liquid is reduced by half, about 3 minutes. Add cream and boil until sauce reduces by half, stirring often, about 3 minutes. Stir in the parsley. Add chicken to sauce, and turn to coat.

In another skillet, melt the remaining 2 tablespoons butter. Add spinach, sauté until heated through, and season with salt and pepper. Arrange spinach on a plate, place the chicken on top of the spinach, and cover with sauce. Makes 4 servings.

Chicken Gruyère with Sautéed Mushrooms

3 tablespoons all-purpose flour
Salt and black pepper, to taste
4 boneless, skinless chicken breasts, pounded thin
6 teaspoons butter, divided
2 cups sliced mushrooms
4 ounces shredded Gruyère or Swiss cheese
Parsley sprigs and cherry tomatoes, for garnish

On a sheet of waxed paper or in shallow dish, combine flour, salt, and pepper; dredge chicken in seasoned flour, coating all sides. In small nonstick skillet, heat 4 teaspoons butter over medium heat until bubbly and hot; add chicken, sprinkle evenly with any remaining seasoned flour, and cook, turning once, until golden brown on both sides. Remove skillet from heat, and transfer chicken to a shallow baking dish; set aside and keep warm.

In same skillet, heat remaining 2 teaspoons butter over medium heat until bubbly and hot; add mushrooms and sauté until lightly browned. Top chicken with mushrooms, then cheese; broil 6 inches from heat source until cheese is melted, 3 to 5 minutes. Serve garnished with parsley springs and tomatoes. Makes 4 servings.

Chicken Hash

1 medium onion, thinly sliced
2 tablespoons butter
4 ounces sliced mushrooms
1 tablespoon chicken bouillon granules
1 teaspoon all-purpose flour
½ cup water
2 cups cooked and chopped chicken
1 tablespoon lemon juice
½ teaspoon sugar
Salt and black pepper, to taste

Cook onions in butter over low heat until soft, being careful not to brown onions. Add mushrooms and cook 2 minutes more. Combine chicken bouillon granules with flour and water; stir into onion mixture. Add chicken and bring to a boil. Remove from heat and add lemon juice, sugar, and salt and pepper to taste. Makes 4 servings.

Chicken in a Bag

1 (4-pound) whole chicken, cut into 8 pieces
2 potatoes, cubed
2 large onions, chopped
½ cup brown sugar
1 cup ketchup
Salt
Black pepper
Garlic powder
Cooking bag

Combine all ingredients in a bag and shake gently until well mixed. Bake at 350° for 2 hours or until chicken is done. Makes 8 servings.

Chicken in Fragrant Spices

6 boneless, skinless chicken breasts
3 garlic cloves, minced
2 tablespoons minced fresh ginger
1 tablespoon ground cumin
½ teaspoon ground turmeric
¼ cup plain nonfat yogurt, stirred until smooth

Make three diagonal slashes in the flesh of each chicken breast. Combine all remaining ingredients. Add the chicken breasts, and coat well with the mixture. Marinate at least 8 hours or up to 48 hours.

Prepare an outside grill with an oiled rack set 4 inches above the heat source. On a gas grill, set the heat to high. Grill the chicken breasts for 3 to 4 minutes on each side, until the chicken is cooked through. Makes 6 servings.

Chicken Jambalaya

1 tablespoon olive oil
1 medium onion, chopped
2 to 3 garlic cloves, minced
¾ pound boneless, skinless chicken breasts, cut in ¾-inch pieces
1 (14½-can) whole plum tomatoes in juice
1 rib celery, cut in ½-inch slices
1 small green bell pepper, chopped
1 scallion, chopped
1 tablespoon tomato paste
1 bay leaf
1 teaspoon dried thyme
¼ teaspoon cayenne pepper
1 cup cooked long-grain brown rice

In a large pot or Dutch oven, heat oil over medium-high heat. Add onion and garlic. Sauté, stirring frequently, until onion is tender but not brown, about 4 minutes. Add chicken and cook, stirring, until pieces are white on all sides. Add tomatoes with liquid, breaking up with spoon. Mix in celery, bell pepper, scallion, and tomato paste. Stir in bay leaf, thyme, and cayenne. Bring to a boil, reduce heat, and simmer until chicken is cooked and sauce has thickened, about 20 minutes. Remove bay leaf. Stir rice into chicken mixture until well combined. Makes 2 servings.

Chicken Kapama

1 (3- to 4-pound) chicken, cut into serving pieces
Salt and black pepper, to taste
¼ teaspoon ground cinnamon
6 tablespoons butter, divided
2 cups canned crushed tomatoes
1 (6-ounce) can tomato paste
1 teaspoon sugar
¾ cup water
3 cinnamon sticks
1 bay leaf
1 cup minced onion
1 tablespoon minced garlic
1 pound macaroni, cooked according to package directions and drained
1 cup grated Parmesan cheese

Sprinkle chicken with salt, pepper, and cinnamon. In a Dutch oven, melt 2 tablespoons butter, and brown chicken until golden on all sides. In a bowl, combine tomatoes, tomato paste, sugar, and water, and pour mixture over chicken. Add cinnamon sticks and bay leaf. In a medium frying pan, melt 2 tablespoons butter, and sauté onion and garlic for 2 minutes. Add to chicken. Bring to a boil, cover, and simmer until chicken is tender, 50 to 60 minutes. Melt remaining butter and pour over macaroni. Place macaroni on a large serving platter. Place chicken and sauce over macaroni, and sprinkle with grated cheese. Makes 6 servings.

Chicken Marsala

4 tablespoons all-purpose flour
Salt and black pepper, to taste
4 large boneless, skinless chicken breasts, cut in half and pounded thin
4 tablespoons butter or olive oil
1 (13-ounce) can chicken broth
1 cup Marsala
3 tablespoons chopped fresh parsley
1 (8-ounce) package sliced mushrooms

Season flour with salt and pepper. Dredge chicken in flour. In large skillet, melt butter or olive oil on low. Increase heat to medium, and brown chicken on each side, about 2 minutes. Remove chicken from pan. Add chicken broth, Marsala, parsley, and mushrooms to skillet, and simmer about 10 minutes. Add chicken and let cook on low about 15 minutes. Makes 4 servings.

Chicken Normandy

Butter-flavored vegetable cooking spray
4 boneless, skinless chicken breasts
Salt and black pepper, to taste
2 medium Granny Smith apples, cored and sliced
6 green onions, sliced
⅔ cup apple cider or unsweetened apple juice
2 teaspoons chicken bouillon granules
1½ teaspoons dried sage
⅔ cup nonfat half-and-half or 2% milk
2 teaspoons all-purpose flour
1¾ teaspoons artificial sweetener
Sage or parsley sprigs for garnish

Spray a large skillet with cooking spray; over medium heat, sauté chicken breasts until browned, 3 to 5 minutes on each side. Season to taste with salt and pepper. Add apples, onions, apple cider, bouillon, and sage to skillet; heat to boiling. Reduce heat and simmer covered until chicken is tender, 10 to 12 minutes. Remove chicken and apples to serving platter.

Continue simmering cider mixture until almost evaporated. Mix half-and-half, flour, and artificial sweetener in a glass measuring cup; pour into skillet. Heat to boiling; boil, stirring constantly, until thickened, about 1 minute. Season to taste with salt and pepper; pour over chicken and apples. Garnish with sage or parsley. Makes 4 servings.

Chicken Parmesan

1½ chopped cups onion
4 garlic cloves, minced
⅓ cup margarine or olive oil
6 cups stewed tomatoes
1 (6-ounce) can tomato paste
½ cup snipped parsley
2 teaspoons salt
3 tablespoons crushed oregano
½ teaspoon crushed thyme
1 teaspoon crushed basil
2 cups water
6 boneless, skinless chicken breasts
⅓ cup butter or margarine
1 cup breadcrumbs
½ cup grated Parmesan cheese
¼ teaspoon salt
Dash pepper
2 eggs, slightly beaten
1 cup sliced or grated mozzarella cheese

Sauté onions and garlic in margarine in a large pot. Add stewed tomatoes, tomato paste, parsley, salt, oregano, thyme, basil, and water. Simmer for 1 hour.

Melt butter or margarine in a baking dish. Combine breadcrumbs, Parmesan cheese, salt, and pepper. Dip chicken pieces in beaten egg, then in crumb mixture. Arrange in baking dish.

Bake for 15 minutes at 400°. Turn chicken pieces over and bake 15 minutes more. Pour tomato sauce over chicken and top with mozzarella cheese; reduce heat to 350°. Continue baking for 30 minutes. Makes 6 servings.

Chicken Pepper Skillet

1 tablespoon vegetable oil
4 skinless, boneless chicken breasts, cut into ½-inch strips
2 garlic cloves, finely minced
3 bell peppers (red, green, and yellow), cut into thin strips
2 medium onions, sliced
1 teaspoon ground cumin
1½ teaspoons dried oregano
2 teaspoons chopped fresh jalapeños
3 tablespoons fresh lemon juice
2 tablespoons chopped fresh parsley
¼ teaspoon salt
Black pepper, to taste

In a large nonstick skillet, heat oil over medium-high heat; add chicken and stir-fry until done and lightly browned, about 3 to 4 minutes. Add garlic and cook 15 seconds, stirring constantly. Add bell peppers, onion, cumin, oregano, and jalapeños. Stir-fry for 2 to 3 minutes or until crisp and tender. Add lemon juice, parsley, salt, and pepper; toss to combine well. Makes 4 servings.

Chicken Piccata

4 boneless, skinless chicken breasts
Salt and black pepper, to taste
1 cup all-purpose flour
6 tablespoons butter, divided
5 tablespoons extra-virgin olive oil, divided
⅓ cup fresh lemon juice
½ cup chicken broth
¼ cup brined capers, rinsed
⅓ cup chopped fresh parsley

Season chicken with salt and pepper. Dredge chicken in flour, and shake off excess. In a large skillet over medium high heat, melt 2 tablespoons of butter with 3 tablespoons olive oil. When butter and oil start to sizzle, add 2 pieces of chicken, and cook for 3 minutes. When chicken is browned, flip and cook other side for 3 minutes. Remove and transfer to plate. Melt 2 more tablespoons butter and add another 2 tablespoons olive oil. When butter and oil start to sizzle, repeat with other 2 pieces of chicken.

Into the pan add the lemon juice, broth, and capers. Return to heat and bring to boil, scraping up browned bits from the pan. Check for seasoning. Return all the chicken to the pan, and simmer for 5 minutes. Remove chicken to platter. Add remaining 2 tablespoons butter to sauce, and whisk vigorously. Pour sauce over chicken, and garnish with parsley. Makes 4 servings.

Chicken Pot Pie

1 pound boneless, skinless chicken, cooked and cut into small pieces
1 (10¾-ounce) can cream of chicken soup
1 (15-ounce) can mixed vegetables, drained
2 deep-dish refrigerated pie shells

Mix chicken, chicken soup, and vegetables. Heat in saucepan until warm. Prepare one pie crust according to package directions. Pour ingredients into shell, place second pie crust on top of mixture, and crimp edges to seal. Bake in 350° oven until crust is done. Makes 4 servings.

Chicken Pot Pie #2

4 cups cooked and chopped chicken
2 cups chicken broth
4 hard-boiled eggs, peeled and chopped
1 (10¾-ounce) can cream of chicken soup
1 (20-ounce) package frozen mixed vegetables, thawed and drained
½ cup butter, melted
1 cup milk
1 cup self-rising flour

Combine chicken, broth, eggs, soup, and vegetables; pour into a 3-quart greased baking dish. Combine butter, milk, and flour; pour over chicken mixture. Bake at 350° for about 1 hour. Makes about 4 servings.

Chicken Pot Pie #3

2 (10¾-ounce) cans cream of potato soup
1 (15-ounce) can mixed vegetables, drained
2 cups cooked and chopped chicken
½ cup milk
½ teaspoon dried thyme
½ teaspoon pepper
2 (9-inch) refrigerated pie crusts
1 egg, slightly beaten

Combine soup, mixed vegetables, chicken, milk, thyme, and pepper in a
bowl; mix well. Spoon into pie crust; top with remaining pie crust; crimp
edges to seal. Cut vents; brush with egg. Bake at 375° for 40 minutes.
Makes 6 servings.

Chicken Pot Pie #4

2 teaspoons olive oil
½ cup plus 2 tablespoons nonfat, low-sodium chicken broth, divided
2 cups sliced mushrooms
1 cup diced red bell pepper
½ cup chopped onion
½ cup chopped celery
2 tablespoons all-purpose flour
½ cup nonfat half-and-half
2 cups cooked and chopped chicken tenders
1 teaspoon minced fresh dill
½ teaspoon salt
¼ teaspoon black pepper
2 low-fat refrigerated crescent rolls

Heat oil and 2 tablespoons chicken broth in medium saucepan. Add mushrooms, bell pepper, onion, and celery. Cook for 5 to 7 minutes, or until vegetables are tender, stirring frequently. Stir in flour; cook for 1 minute. Stir in remaining ½ cup chicken broth; cook and stir until liquid thickens. Reduce heat and stir in half-and-half. Add cooked chicken, dill, salt, and pepper. Spoon mixture into greased 1-quart casserole. Roll out dough and place on top of chicken mixture. Bake at 375° for 15 to 20 minutes, or until topping is golden and filling is bubbly. Makes 4 servings.

Chicken Ratatouille

3 tablespoons olive oil
3 boneless, skinless chicken breasts, cut into strips
1 zucchini, sliced
1 eggplant, cubed
1 onion, sliced
1 bell pepper, chopped
1 (8-ounce) package sliced mushrooms
2 teaspoons garlic, minced
2 teaspoons Italian seasoning
Salt and black pepper, to taste
1 (14-ounce) can diced tomatoes
2 cups cooked rice

Heat olive oil in large skillet; add chicken and cook several minutes. Add zucchini, eggplant, onion, bell pepper, mushrooms, garlic, Italian seasoning, salt, and pepper. Cook until chicken is done and vegetables are tender. Add tomatoes and cook until heated through. Serve over rice. Makes 4 servings.

Chicken Sardou

4 boneless, skinless chicken breasts
½ teaspoon dried oregano
Salt and black pepper, to taste
1 tablespoon olive oil
1 (8-ounce) jar marinated artichoke hearts, drained and chopped
½ cup grated Parmesan cheese

Season chicken with oregano, salt, and pepper. Cook in hot oil in ovenproof skillet until thoroughly cooked. Top each cooked chicken breast with chopped artichoke hearts and Parmesan cheese; run under a preheated broiler until cheese is melted and golden brown. Makes 4 servings.

Chicken Spaghetti

2 pounds boneless, skinless chicken breasts or thighs
1 (1-ounce) package spaghetti mix
2 garlic cloves, minced
2 onions, chopped
1 (14-ounce) can crushed tomatoes
1 (8-ounce) can tomato sauce
1 (6-ounce) can tomato paste
½ teaspoon red pepper flakes
½ teaspoon Italian seasoning
½ teaspoon black pepper
½ teaspoon dried oregano
1 (16-ounce) package dried angel hair pasta, cooked
1 cup shredded mozzarella cheese

Place chicken in a slow cooker, followed by all other ingredients except pasta and cheese. Cook on low for 6 to 8 hours. Near the end of cooking time, break up chicken into small pieces and stir. Serve over pasta and sprinkle with cheese. Makes 6 to 8 servings.

Chicken Strips with Garlic and Butter Sauce

2 to 3 pounds breaded chicken strips
Oil
¼ cup butter
2 garlic cloves, chopped
3 cups chicken broth, divided
1 to 2 teaspoons parsley flakes, divided

Lightly brown chicken strips in oil. Remove chicken and drain oil. Melt butter and sauté chopped garlic cloves in same frying pan. Add chicken and 1½ cups of chicken broth. Add parsley and cook over low heat. Liquid will begin to thicken. Add more liquid and continue simmering for 30 to 45 minutes, adding more chicken broth as it thickens. Sprinkle parsley on top. Makes 8 to 12 servings.

Chicken Stroganoff

1 cup light sour cream
1 tablespoon all-purpose flour
1 (1-ounce) package chicken gravy mix
1 cup water
1 pound boneless, skinless chicken breasts, cut into 1-inch cubes
1 (16-ounce) bag frozen mixed vegetables, thawed and drained

In a slow cooker, mix sour cream, flour, gravy mix, and water; stir with wire whisk until well blended. Add chicken to slow cooker. Stir in vegetables and cover. Cook on low for 4 hours, until chicken is tender. Turn heat to high, and cook for 1 hour longer, until sauce is thickened and chicken is thoroughly cooked. Makes 4 servings.

Chicken Tacos

1 fryer chicken, skinned if desired
1 (18-ounce) jar salsa
2 tablespoons taco seasoning mix
Taco shells

Place chicken in a slow cooker. In a medium bowl, combine salsa and taco seasoning, and mix to blend. Pour over top of chicken. Remove chicken and let cool slightly. Cover and cook on low for 6 to 8 hours, until chicken is tender and thoroughly cooked.

Remove skin and bones from chicken. Shred meat and stir back into liquid in slow cooker. Cook 20 to 30 minutes longer until thoroughly heated. Serve in taco shells. Makes 4 to 6 servings.

Chicken Tetrazzini

1 (10¾-ounce) can low-fat cream of chicken soup
¼ cup water
½ cup grated Parmesan cheese
4 cups cooked spaghetti
1½ cups cooked and chopped chicken
2 tablespoons chopped fresh parsley, or 2 teaspoons dried parsley

In a skillet, combine soup, water, and cheese over low heat, stirring occasionally, until cheese is melted, about 3 minutes. Add cooked spaghetti, chicken, and parsley to skillet. Warm thoroughly over low heat, stirring occasionally, approximately 10 minutes. Makes 4 servings.

Chicken Tortillas

1 whole chicken, cooked and removed from bone
1 (10¾-ounce) can cream of chicken soup
½ cup green chile salsa
2 tablespoons quick-cooking tapioca
12 corn tortillas
1 medium onion, chopped
1½ cups grated Monterey Jack cheese
Black olives

Tear chicken into bite-size pieces, and mix with soup, chili, salsa, and tapioca. Line bottom of a slow cooker with 3 corn tortillas, torn into bite-size pieces. Add ⅓ of the chicken mixture. Sprinkle with ⅓ of the onion and ⅓ of the grated cheese. Repeat with layers of tortillas, chicken mixture, onions, and cheese. Cover and cook on low 6 to 8 hours. Garnish with sliced black olives. Makes 12 servings.

Chicken with Caramelized Onions

4 teaspoons olive oil or canola oil, divided
1 large yellow or white onion, thinly sliced
½ teaspoon salt, divided
⅓ cup chicken broth
½ tablespoon balsamic vinegar
1 teaspoon whole-grain mustard
¼ teaspoon freshly ground black pepper, divided
4 boneless, skinless chicken breasts
1½ tablespoons chopped fresh thyme

In a large nonstick frying pan, warm 1 tablespoon oil over medium-low heat. Add onion and cook, stirring frequently, until golden brown, about 20 minutes (do not let the onion burn). Stir in ¼ teaspoon salt. In a small saucepan over medium-low heat, combine broth, vinegar, and mustard; whisk to blend. Add onion, and ⅛ teaspoon black pepper; cook until liquid is reduced by half, 4 to 5 minutes. Remove from heat and keep warm.

Place the chicken breasts between 2 sheets of heavy-duty plastic wrap. With a meat mallet or rolling pin, pound the breasts to an even ¼-inch thickness. Sprinkle the pounded chicken with the remaining salt and pepper. Place the chopped thyme in a shallow dish. Dredge the chicken in the thyme, pressing to make the leaves stick. In the same large nonstick pan used for the onion, warm the remaining 1 teaspoon oil over medium-high heat. Add the chicken, and cook, turning once, until opaque throughout, about 2 to 3 minutes per side. To serve, place the chicken on individual plates, and top with the onion sauce. Makes 4 servings.

Chicken with Garlic Sauce

1½ pounds boneless, skinless chicken breast, cut into small pieces
2 tablespoons garlic powder
½ cup melted butter
2 tablespoons lemon juice
5 garlic cloves, chopped
1 small onion, chopped
6 to 8 ounces sliced mushrooms
Salt and black pepper, to taste
3 tablespoons soy sauce
Dash dried oregano
Dash dried parsley
Paprika
2 tablespoons breadcrumbs
Cooked rice

Season chicken pieces with garlic powder. Place in shallow baking dish. Add
butter, lemon juice, garlic, onion, mushrooms, salt, pepper, and soy sauce.
Very lightly sprinkle with oregano and parsley. Generously cover with
paprika. Bake at 350° for approximately 15 minutes. Turn chicken, sprinkle
with breadcrumbs, and cover with more paprika. Bake 15 minutes more, or
until chicken browns. Serve over rice. Makes 4 servings.

Chicken with Mushrooms and Basil

3 cups sliced fresh mushrooms, cooked
1 onion, chopped and cooked
2 garlic cloves, minced
Salt and black pepper, to taste
2¼ pounds boneless, skinless chicken pieces
1 cup chicken stock
1 (6-ounce) can tomato paste
2 tablespoons quick-cooking tapioca
2 teaspoons sugar
1½ teaspoons dried basil, crushed
Cooked noodles
2 tablespoons grated Parmesan cheese

Combine mushrooms, onion, garlic, salt, and pepper in a slow cooker.
Arrange chicken pieces over vegetables. Combine stock, next four
ingredients, salt, and pepper in a bowl. Pour over chicken. Cover and cook
on low 7 to 8 hours or on high about 4 hours. Serve over noodles, sprinkled
with Parmesan cheese. Makes 8 servings.

Chicken with Tomato Sauce and Mushrooms

1 teaspoon paprika
1 teaspoon garlic powder
Salt and black pepper, to taste
3 pounds boneless, skinless chicken breasts
1 (6-ounce) can tomato paste
1 cup water
1 (8-ounce) can sliced mushrooms
Cooked rice

Combine paprika, garlic powder, salt, and pepper. Sprinkle spice mixture on each piece of chicken. Place chicken in a slow cooker. Mix tomato paste and water together. Pour over chicken. Add sliced mushrooms. Cover and cook on low for 7 to 9 hours. Serve over rice. Makes 12 servings.

Chipped Beef Chicken

6 boneless, skinless chicken breasts
1 (5-ounce) jar chipped beef, chopped
1 (10¾-ounce) can cream of mushroom soup
1 cup sour cream
⅓ cup milk

Place chicken in large greased baking dish. Combine chipped beef, soup, sour cream, and milk; pour over chicken. Bake at 400° for about 30 minutes. Makes 6 servings.

Chipped Beef Chicken with Bacon and Cheese

6 boneless, skinless chicken breasts
1 (5-ounce) jar chipped beef, chopped
6 slices bacon, cooked and crumbled
1 (10¼-ounce) can cream of mushroom soup
1 cup sour cream
⅓ cup milk
1 cup shredded Cheddar cheese

Place chicken in large greased baking dish. Combine chipped beef, bacon, soup, sour cream, and milk; pour over chicken. Sprinkle with shredded cheese. Bake at 400° for about 30 minutes. Makes 6 servings.

Cilantro Pesto Chicken and Pasta

1 cup fresh cilantro leaves
2½ tablespoons extra virgin olive oil
2 tablespoons sliced, toasted almonds
3 tablespoons chopped garlic
1½ teaspoons lime juice
1 cup shredded Asiago cheese, divided
1½ teaspoons salt
¼ cup chicken broth
8 ounces dried linguine pasta, cooked al dente
2 cups cooked and chopped chicken
1 cup julienned sun-dried tomatoes

In a blender, combine the cilantro, olive oil, almonds, garlic, lime juice, ½ cup Asiago, salt, and chicken broth. Blend on low speed for 2 minutes. Set aside. In a large saucepan, heat pasta, chicken, and pesto sauce over medium heat for 2 minutes. Pour into serving bowls. Top with remaining Asiago and sun-dried tomatoes. Makes 4 servings.

Citrus Chicken

1 cup grapefruit juice
¼ cup frozen orange juice concentrate, thawed
2 tablespoons honey
1 tablespoon fresh lemon juice
2 teaspoons peeled and grated ginger
⅛ teaspoon red pepper flakes
4 boneless, skinless chicken breasts
1 tablespoon reduced-calorie margarine
¼ teaspoon salt

In a medium nonmetallic bowl, stir together grapefruit juice, orange juice concentrate, honey, lemon juice, ginger, and red pepper flakes. Remove and set aside 1 cup juice mixture. Add chicken pieces to the juice mixture remaining in the bowl, turning to coat. Let marinate for 15 minutes, turning occasionally.

Heat a 12-inch nonstick skillet over medium heat. Remove from heat, and lightly spray with vegetable oil spray (being careful not to spray near a gas flame). Remove the chicken from the marinade; discard the marinade. Cook the chicken for 5 minutes on each side, or until no longer pink in the center. Place on a plate. Stir reserved 1 cup juice mixture into pan residue. Increase heat to high, and bring to a boil. Boil for 3 minutes, or until mixture is reduced to ½ cup, scraping the bottom and sides of the pan. Remove from heat, stir in the margarine and salt, and pour over the chicken. Makes 4 servings.

Cola Chicken

6 boneless, skinless chicken breasts
1 cup ketchup
1 cup cola beverage
2 tablespoons Worcestershire sauce
2 tablespoons grape jelly

Place chicken in greased baking pan. Combine remaining ingredients, and spread over chicken. Bake at 400° for about 30 minutes. Makes 6 servings.

Country Chicken

1 (2½- to 3-pound) chicken, cut into 8 pieces, skin removed
2 teaspoons curry powder
½ teaspoon salt
¼ to ½ teaspoon cayenne pepper
1 tablespoon olive oil
1 medium onion, cut into thin wedges
2 garlic cloves, minced
1 large green bell pepper, cut into 1-inch pieces
1 (14½-ounce) can diced tomatoes with juice
¼ cup dried currants or raisins
½ teaspoon dried thyme
2 tablespoons sliced almonds

Sprinkle chicken pieces with curry powder, salt, and cayenne. Heat oil in a large nonstick skillet. Brown chicken in oil on all sides, about 10 minutes. Remove and set aside. Sauté onion and garlic in same skillet for 3 minutes. Add bell pepper, tomatoes with liquid, currants, and thyme. Bring to a boil.

Return chicken to skillet; reduce heat. Cover and simmer until chicken is tender, about 15 minutes, spooning juices over chicken occasionally. While chicken is cooking, toast almonds in a small skillet over medium heat for about 3 minutes until slightly browned and fragrant. Sprinkle dish with toasted almonds at serving time. Makes 8 servings.

Creamed Chicken

3 tablespoons butter
4 tablespoons all-purpose flour
1 cup chicken stock
1 cup milk
2 cups cooked and chopped chicken
3 hard-boiled eggs, peeled and chopped
½ teaspoon salt
½ teaspoon black pepper

Melt butter; add flour and stir over low heat until well blended. Add chicken stock and milk. Cook over low heat until thickened and smooth. Add chopped chicken and eggs; season with salt and pepper. Serve over hot biscuits. Makes 4 servings.

Cream of Mushroom Chicken with Almonds

6 boneless, skinless chicken breasts
½ cup chicken broth
1 (10¾-ounce) can cream of mushroom soup
½ pint sour cream
Sliced almonds

Place the chicken breasts in the bottom of a slow cooker. Mix together the broth, soup, and sour cream. Pour over the chicken. Cover and cook for 8 hours on low heat. Sprinkle with almonds before serving. Makes 6 servings.

Creamy Baked Chicken

6 boneless, skinless chicken breasts
1 (10¾-ounce) can cream of chicken soup
1 cup sour cream
½ cup grated Parmesan cheese

Place chicken breasts in greased baking dish. Combine soup, sour cream, and cheese. Pour over chicken, turning to coat. Bake at 400° for about 30 minutes. Makes 6 servings.

Creamy Baked Chicken and Asparagus

6 boneless, skinless chicken breasts
½ bunch asparagus, trimmed and cut into 1-inch pieces
1 (10¾-ounce) can cream of asparagus soup
1 cup sour cream
½ cup grated Parmesan cheese

Place chicken breasts and asparagus in greased baking dish. Combine soup, sour cream, and cheese. Pour over chicken, turning to coat. Bake at 400° for about 30 minutes. Makes 6 servings.

Creamy Baked Chicken and Broccoli

6 boneless, skinless chicken breasts
1 (10-ounce) package frozen chopped broccoli, thawed and drained
1 (10¾-ounce) can cream of broccoli soup
1 cup sour cream
½ cup shredded Cheddar cheese

Place chicken breasts and broccoli in greased baking dish. Combine soup, sour cream, and cheese. Pour over chicken, turning to coat. Bake at 400° for about 30 minutes. Makes 6 servings.

Creamy Baked Chicken with Mushrooms

6 boneless, skinless chicken breasts
1 (8-ounce) package sliced mushrooms
1 (10¾-ounce) can cream of mushroom soup
1 cup sour cream
½ cup grated Parmesan cheese

Place chicken breasts and mushrooms in greased baking dish. Combine soup, sour cream, and cheese. Pour over chicken, turning to coat. Bake at 400° for about 30 minutes. Makes 6 servings.

Creamy Chicken

6 to 8 chicken pieces, on the bone
1 cup evaporated milk
1 (10¾-ounce) can cream of mushroom soup
Salt and pepper, to taste
Paprika

Place chicken in bottom of a slow cooker. Mix together evaporated milk and soup. Pour over chicken. Sprinkle with salt, pepper, and paprika. Cover and cook on low for 8 hours. Makes 6 to 8 servings.

Creamy Chicken Casserole

1½ pounds boneless, skinless chicken breasts
6 carrots, sliced
1 (15-ounce) can green beans, drained
2 (10¾-ounce) cans cream of mushroom soup
2 tablespoons mayonnaise
½ cup shredded Cheddar cheese

Place chicken in bottom of a slow cooker. Mix carrots, green beans, mushroom soup, and mayonnaise. Pour over chicken. Cover and cook for 8 to 10 hours on low. Sprinkle with Cheddar cheese before serving. Makes 4 servings.

Creamy Curried Chicken over Rice

1 onion, chopped
2 tablespoons butter
3 tablespoons all-purpose flour
1 to 2 teaspoons curry powder, or to taste
1 cup chicken broth
½ cup cream
1½ cups cooked and chopped chicken
Salt and black pepper, to taste
2 cups cooked rice
Chopped green onion, shredded coconut, chopped apples, raisins, chopped peanuts, mango chutney

Cook onion in butter in medium saucepan over medium heat about 5 minutes or until soft. Stir in flour and curry powder, and cook, stirring constantly, for 3 minutes. Gradually add chicken broth and cream, and cook until thick and bubbly, stirring constantly. Add chicken, salt, and pepper, and cook until heated through. Serve over rice with desired accompaniments. Makes 4 servings.

Creamy Italian Chicken

2 pounds boneless, skinless chicken breasts, cut into strips
¼ cup butter, melted
1 (8-ounce) container cream cheese with chives, softened
1 (10¾-ounce) can condensed golden cream of mushroom soup
1 (0.7-ounce) package Italian dressing mix
½ cup water
2 cups cooked rice or noodles

Place chicken in bottom of a slow cooker. In a medium bowl, combine butter, cream cheese, soup, dressing mix, and water, and stir until blended. Pour over chicken. Cover and cook on low for 6 to 8 hours. Stir well, and serve over pasta or rice. Makes 4 to 6 servings.

Crispy Chicken

1 cup cornflakes
¼ teaspoon dried thyme
¼ teaspoon black pepper
4 boneless, skinless chicken breasts
1 tablespoon margarine, melted

Crush the cornflakes between two sheets of waxed paper, and mix with thyme and pepper. Place the chicken, breast-side up, in a baking pan. Brush the chicken with the melted margarine. Sprinkle the cornflakes on top of the chicken breasts, cover lightly with foil, and bake at 400° for 30 minutes. Carefully remove foil; bake uncovered for another 15 minutes. Makes 4 servings.

Curried Chicken

4 chicken breasts, on the bone
½ cup honey
½ cup Dijon mustard
2 tablespoons soy sauce
¼ teaspoon curry powder

Place all ingredients in a slow cooker. Cover and cook on low for 8 hours. Makes 4 servings.

Dijon Chicken

¼ cup Dijon mustard
2 tablespoons olive oil
1 tablespoon lemon juice
1 teaspoon garlic salt
1 teaspoon dried oregano
4 boneless, skinless chicken breasts

Combine Dijon mustard, olive oil, lemon juice, garlic salt, and oregano. Spread over chicken breasts. Bake on a greased baking sheet at 400° for about 30 minutes. Makes 4 servings.

Easy Chicken Burritos

3 cups cooked and chopped chicken
1 (10¾-ounce) can cream of chicken soup
1 cup salsa
4 (10-inch) flour tortillas
1 cup shredded Monterey Jack cheese
2 green onions, chopped

Combine chicken, soup, and salsa in a saucepan, and cook until heated through. Roll up in tortillas and place seam-side down in a greased baking dish. Sprinkle with cheese and green onions. Bake at 350° for about 20 minutes, just until cheese is melted. Makes 4 servings.

Easy Chicken Cordon Bleu

4 boneless, skinless chicken breasts
½ teaspoon dried thyme
Salt and black pepper, to taste
1 tablespoon olive oil
4 slices ham
4 slices Swiss cheese

Season chicken with thyme, salt, and pepper. Cook in hot oil in ovenproof skillet until done. Top each breast with 1 slice ham and 1 slice Swiss cheese. Run under preheated broiler until cheese is melted and golden brown. Makes 4 servings.

Easy Chicken Enchiladas

3 cups cooked and chopped chicken
1 (10¾-ounce) can cream of chicken soup
1 cup salsa
8 (6-inch) corn tortillas
1 can enchilada sauce
1 cup shredded Cheddar cheese

Combine chicken, soup, and salsa in a saucepan, and cook until heated through. Roll up in tortillas, and place seam-side down in a greased baking dish. Cover with enchilada sauce and Cheddar cheese. Bake at 350° for about 20 minutes. Makes 4 servings.

Easy Chicken Kiev

½ cup butter, softened
1 teaspoon garlic salt
1 teaspoon dried parsley
4 boneless, skinless chicken breasts, pounded thin
½ cup all-purpose flour
2 eggs, beaten
1 cup breadcrumbs
¼ cup vegetable oil

Combine butter, garlic salt, and parsley, mixing well. Divide into 4 equal pieces and freeze. Place 1 frozen butter piece in center of each piece of chicken; roll up and secure with toothpicks. Dredge each piece in flour, dip in egg, and roll in breadcrumbs. In an ovenproof skillet, brown in hot oil on all sides. Transfer to oven. Bake at 400° for about 20 minutes. Makes 4 servings.

Easy Chicken Parmesan

6 frozen fully cooked breaded boneless chicken breasts, thawed
1 (28-ounce) jar pasta sauce
2 cups shredded mozzarella cheese
½ cup grated Parmesan cheese

Arrange chicken breasts in a greased baking dish; pour sauce evenly over chicken. Sprinkle cheeses over sauce. Bake at 350° for about 30 minutes, or until chicken is heated through and cheese is melted and bubbly. Makes 6 servings.

Easy Chicken Quesadillas

3 cups cooked and chopped chicken
1 (10¾-ounce) can cream of chicken soup
1 cup salsa
4 (8-inch) flour tortillas
1 cup shredded Cheddar cheese
1 cup shredded Monterey Jack cheese
2 tablespoons butter

Combine chicken, soup, and salsa in a saucepan, and cook until heated through. Place ¼ of chicken mixture on each tortilla; sprinkle evenly with cheeses. Fold over like an omelet. Melt butter in large skillet, and cook quesadillas one at a time, turning once, until cheese is melted and tortilla is crisp. Makes 4 servings.

Easy Chicken Saltimbocca

4 boneless, skinless chicken breasts
½ teaspoon dried sage
Salt and black pepper, to taste
1 tablespoon olive oil
4 slices prosciutto
½ cup shredded mozzarella cheese

Season chicken with sage, salt, and pepper. Cook in hot oil in ovenproof skillet until done. Top each breast with 1 slice prosciutto and 2 tablespoons shredded cheese; run under preheated broiler until cheese is melted and golden brown. Makes 4 servings.

Eggplant Chicken

6 tablespoons olive oil
3 garlic cloves, chopped
1 Japanese eggplant, cut into ⅛-inch slices
2 boneless, skinless chicken breasts, thinly sliced
4 red chile peppers
12 basil leaves
2 tablespoons yellow bean sauce

In a large skillet, heat oil over medium heat. Add garlic and stir-fry until fragrant, about 1 minute. Add eggplant and chicken, and cook for 5 to 7 minutes, or until chicken is done. Add red chile peppers, basil leaves, and yellow bean sauce; mix well. Serve immediately. Makes 4 servings.

Fast and Easy Chicken and Dumplings

2 chicken breasts, on the bone
1 quart chicken broth
2 (10-ounce) cans refrigerated biscuit dough
½ cup all-purpose flour
Salt and black pepper, to taste

Simmer chicken in broth until done; remove from broth. Discard bone and skin from chicken. Cut each piece of biscuit dough into 3 pieces and drop into the chicken broth, stirring with a fork. Add more water if needed. Cover and simmer 12 to 15 minutes.

To thicken, stir 1 cup water into ½ cup flour. Gradually add to broth, mixing well. Return chicken to dumplings, add salt and pepper. Makes 2 servings.

Fast and Easy Chicken Casserole

⅔ cup quick-cooking rice
1 (10¾-ounce) can cream of mushroom soup
2 chicken breasts, on the bone

Place the rice in a casserole dish. Add cream of mushroom soup. Place
chicken breasts on top. Bake uncovered at 350° for 1 to 1½ hours. Makes 2
servings.

Fast Chicken and Rice Casserole

1 (3-pound) whole chicken, cooked and deboned
3 cups chicken broth
1 (1-ounce) package onion soup mix
2 cups quick-cooking rice

Mix all ingredients together, and place in a casserole. Bake covered for 1
hour at 350°. Makes 4 to 6 servings.

Fast Chicken and Vegetable Stir-Fry

4 to 6 boneless, skinless chicken breasts, cut into 1-inch cubes
1 (1-pound) package mixed vegetables
1 (10¾-ounce) can Cheddar cheese soup
Cajun spice

Brown chicken in skillet; season to taste. Add vegetables and stir-fry until
tender. Add soup and spice; mix thoroughly. Simmer until hot. Makes 4 to 6
servings.

Fast 'n' Fancy Cornish Hens

1 box quick-cooking wild rice mix
2 (10¾-ounce) cans tomato soup
2 to 3 Cornish hens, cleaned and halved
1 (10¾-ounce) can golden mushroom soup

In a medium bowl, mix rice together with tomato soup and 1½ cans of water. Pour into a baking dish. Top with Cornish hens. Pour mushroom soup over hens. Cover with foil. Bake at 350° for 1 hour. Uncover and bake 15 minutes more until browned. Makes 2 to 3 servings.

Feta-Stuffed Chicken

4 ounces feta cheese, crumbled
4 sun-dried tomatoes, chopped
1 teaspoon olive oil
½ teaspoon dried basil
4 boneless, skinless chicken breasts, pounded to ¼-inch thickness

In a bowl, combine cheese, tomatoes, olive oil, and basil. Place ¼ of cheese mixture in the center of each chicken breast, and fold in half. Place in a small greased dish, and bake for 30 minutes at 350°, or until chicken is no longer pink and juices run clear. Makes 4 servings.

Forgotten Chicken

1 (3½-pound) whole fryer chicken, at room temperature
¼ cup butter, softened
Salt and black pepper, to taste

Rub chicken all over with butter; sprinkle with salt and pepper. Bake at 300° for 3 hours. Makes 4 servings.

Fried Chicken

1 (3- to 4-pound) chicken, cut into pieces
1 teaspoon salt
1 teaspoon black pepper
2 cups buttermilk
2 cups all-purpose flour
1 teaspoon garlic powder
1 teaspoon paprika
Vegetable oil

Season chicken with salt and pepper. In a large dish, pour buttermilk over chicken. Allow to soak in refrigerator for 2 hours. Combine flour, garlic powder, and paprika. Dredge chicken in flour mixture. Fry, a few pieces at a time, in preheated oil until golden brown, 8 to 10 minutes for white meat and 12 to 14 minutes for dark meat. Remove from oil and drain. Makes 4 servings.

Garlic and Citrus Chicken

1 (5- to 6-pound) chicken
Salt and black pepper, to taste
1 orange, quartered
1 lemon, quartered
1 head garlic, halved crosswise, plus 3 garlic cloves, chopped
2 (14-ounce) cans chicken broth
¼ cup frozen orange juice concentrate, thawed
¼ cup fresh lemon juice
2 tablespoons olive oil
1 tablespoon chopped fresh oregano leaves

Rinse chicken, pat dry, and sprinkle cavity with salt and pepper. Stuff cavity with the orange, lemon, and garlic halves. Tie legs together with kitchen string to help hold its shape. Sprinkle with salt and pepper.

Place a rack in a large roasting pan. Place chicken, breast-side up, on the rack. Roast at 400° in the center of the oven for 1 hour, basting with broth occasionally and adding some broth to the pan, if necessary, to prevent the pan drippings from burning. Whisk orange juice, lemon juice, oil, oregano, and garlic in a medium bowl to blend. Brush some of juice mixture over chicken, and continue roasting until meat registers at 170°, basting occasionally with the juice mixture and adding broth to the pan, about 45 minutes longer. Transfer chicken to a platter. Tent with foil.

Place the same roasting pan over medium-low heat. Whisk in any remaining broth and simmer until sauce is reduced to 1 cup, stirring often, about 3 minutes. Strain into a 2-cup glass measuring cup, and discard the solids. Spoon fat from the top of the sauce. Serve chicken with pan sauce. Makes 8 to 10 servings.

Garlic Chicken Pizza

1 boneless, skinless chicken breast half
2 tablespoons butter, softened
2 garlic cloves, minced
½ teaspoon dried basil
2 tablespoons chopped green onion
1 (10-ounce) can refrigerated pizza crust dough
½ cup Ricotta cheese
2 Roma plum tomatoes, diced
½ cup chopped fresh cilantro
¼ cup grated Parmesan cheese

Place chicken breast in a saucepan and cover with water. Bring to a boil and cook until the chicken is no longer pink, about 20 minutes. Drain and slice chicken into strips.

Melt butter in a skillet over medium heat. Add the garlic, basil, and onion and cook for 2 to 3 minutes. Pour into a dish and refrigerate it until it sets.

Roll pizza dough flat. Place it on a baking sheet, and evenly spread herb butter over the surface. Spread the chicken strips over the pizza, then sprinkle with Ricotta. Top with slices of tomatoes, cilantro, and Parmesan. Bake at 350° for 15 to 20 minutes. Makes 8 servings.

Garlic Pepper Chicken

4 chicken leg quarters
2 tablespoons minced garlic
2 teaspoons black pepper
1 (15-ounce) can zucchini with tomato sauce
½ cup shredded mozzarella cheese

Place chicken in a slow cooker. Sprinkle with garlic and pepper. Pour zucchini with tomato sauce over chicken. Cook for 6 hours on high. Sprinkle with cheese, and cook until cheese melts, about 30 minutes. Makes 4 servings.

General Tso's Chicken

1 large egg white
3 tablespoons cornstarch, divided
3 tablespoons rice vinegar, divided
3 tablespoons soy sauce, divided
1 pound boneless, skinless chicken thighs, cut into 1-inch cubes
4 tablespoons chicken broth, divided
2 teaspoons sugar
Vegetable oil for frying
12 dried red chile peppers
1 tablespoon minced garlic
1 tablespoon minced ginger
½ teaspoon red pepper flakes
½ cup sliced green onions plus more for garnish
½ cup roughly chopped lightly toasted cashews
Cooked rice

In a bowl, whisk together egg white, 2 tablespoons cornstarch, 2 tablespoons rice vinegar, and 1 tablespoon soy sauce. Add chicken and toss to coat. Cover and marinate in the refrigerator for up to 2 hours.

In another bowl, whisk remaining 1 tablespoon cornstarch with 1 tablespoon chicken broth until smooth. Add the remaining 3 tablespoons chicken broth, 1 tablespoon rice vinegar, 1 tablespoon soy sauce, and sugar, and whisk to combine. Set aside until ready to finish the dish.

In a large wok or pot, heat enough oil to come 3 inches up the sides to 350°. Remove the chicken from the marinade, and carefully slide into the hot oil. Fry, turning, until golden brown and cooked through, about 2 minutes. Remove and drain on paper towels.

Discard all but about 1 tablespoon of the oil from the wok. Add the chile peppers and stir-fry until nearly black. Add the garlic, ginger, red pepper flakes, and green onions. Stir-fry until fragrant, about 15 seconds. Add reserved broth, bring to a boil, and cook, stirring, until the sauce thickens, about 1 minute. Remove from heat.

Arrange chicken on a platter and pour sauce over it. Garnish with cashews and additional green onions. Serve with rice. Makes 4 servings.

Greek Chicken

6 boneless, skinless chicken breasts
Butter
3 tablespoons lemon juice
3 tablespoons olive oil
1½ cups chicken broth
½ teaspoon dried oregano
2 garlic cloves, minced
Salt and black pepper, to taste

Arrange chicken in a large baking dish with 1 pat of butter for each piece of chicken. Mix lemon juice, olive oil, and broth together with oregano, garlic, salt, and pepper. Pour over chicken. Bake 30 minutes at 450° until brown, turning occasionally, basting several times. Cover with tin foil and reduce heat to 350° for approximately 15 minutes. Makes 6 servings.

Grilled Caribbean Chicken Breasts

¼ cup freshly squeezed orange juice
1 teaspoon grated orange zest
1 tablespoon olive oil
1 tablespoon fresh lime juice
1 teaspoon minced ginger
2 garlic cloves, minced
¼ teaspoon hot pepper sauce
½ teaspoon minced fresh oregano
6 boneless, skinless chicken breasts

In a blender, combine all ingredients except chicken. Pour over chicken breasts, and marinate in refrigerator at least 2 hours or up to 48 hours. Grill or broil chicken for about 6 minutes per side, until no trace of pink remains. Makes 6 servings.

Grilled Chicken Tacos

⅓ cup olive or vegetable oil
¼ cup fresh lime juice
4 garlic cloves, minced
1 tablespoon minced fresh parsley
1 teaspoon ground cumin
1 teaspoon dried oregano
½ teaspoon black pepper
4 boneless, skinless chicken breasts
6 (8-inch) flour tortillas or taco shells, warmed
Toppings, to taste

In a large resealable plastic bag or shallow glass container, combine first 7 ingredients. Add chicken and turn to coat. Seal or cover, and refrigerate 8 hours or overnight, turning occasionally. Drain and discard marinade. Grill chicken uncovered over medium heat for 5 to 7 minutes on each side, or until juices run clear. Cut into thin strips; serve in tortillas or taco shells with desired toppings. Makes 4 servings.

Grilled Garlic Chicken

1 (4-pound) chicken, cut into 8 pieces, backbone removed
½ bunch scallions, minced
3 garlic cloves, finely chopped
1 cup orange juice
2 tablespoons cider vinegar
2 teaspoons dried oregano
2 teaspoons kosher salt
1 teaspoon red pepper flakes

Place chicken pieces in a large resealable plastic bags and add the rest of ingredients. Seal bag and shake to mix. Refrigerate at least 1 hour or overnight. Grill over medium heat, skin-side up, for 20 minutes. Turn the pieces and cook an additional 15 to 20 minutes, or until no longer pink inside. Makes 8 servings.

Herbed Chicken and Rice

1 pound boneless, skinless chicken breasts, cut into 1-inch strips
1 tablespoon butter or margarine
2 large carrots, shredded
1 small onion, chopped
2 cups water
¼ teaspoon dried marjoram
¼ teaspoon dried thyme
⅛ teaspoon dried rosemary
⅛ teaspoon ground sage
2 cups instant rice
½ cup chopped walnuts

In a skillet, sauté chicken in butter for 3 to 4 minutes. Add carrots and onion; sauté until tender. Add water and seasonings; bring to a boil. Stir in the rice. Cover and remove from the heat; let stand for 5 minutes. Sprinkle with walnuts. Makes 4 servings.

Honey-Glazed Indian Chicken

¼ cup butter, melted
¼ cup honey
¼ cup coarse-grain mustard
1 tablespoon curry powder
1 teaspoon ground cinnamon
Dash cayenne pepper
6 boneless, skinless chicken breasts

Combine butter, honey, mustard, curry powder, cinnamon, and cayenne pepper. Spread over chicken breasts. Bake on a greased baking sheet at 400° for about 30 minutes. Makes 6 servings.

Hunan Chicken

1½ **pounds boneless, skinless chicken breasts, cut into 1-inch cubes**
1 **egg white, lightly beaten**
1 **tablespoon all-purpose flour**
1 **tablespoon vegetable oil**
2 **green onions, chopped**
1 **teaspoon ground ginger**
1 **teaspoon soy sauce**
4 **teaspoons sugar**
4 **teaspoons rice vinegar**
1 **tablespoon ketchup**
1 **teaspoon cornstarch**
Cooked rice

Dip chicken pieces in egg white, and sprinkle with flour. Warm oil over medium-high heat, and stir-fry chicken in oil until done. Add green onions and ginger, continue to stir-fry. Combine soy sauce, sugar, vinegar, ketchup, and cornstarch. Add to chicken mixture. Cook until thickened and warmed through. Serve with rice. Makes 4 servings.

Indian Chicken

1 cup plain nonfat yogurt
1 tablespoon finely minced or grated ginger
2 large garlic cloves, minced
1 tablespoon paprika
1 teaspoon ground coriander
1 teaspoon ground cumin
1 teaspoon black pepper
½ teaspoon cayenne pepper
8 boneless, skinless chicken breasts

In a small bowl, combine all ingredients except chicken. Place chicken in a flat dish, and cover evenly with yogurt marinade. Refrigerate the chicken for at least 6 hours and up to one day. Preheat the oven broiler. Spray a broiler rack with nonstick cooking spray. Place chicken on rack, broiling 10 to 15 minutes per side, until juices run clear when pierced with a fork. Makes 8 servings.

Island Chicken

2 pounds chicken parts
1 (8-ounce) can pineapple chunks in heavy syrup, drained, liquid
   reserved
1 (10-ounce) can chicken broth
¼ cup vinegar
2 tablespoons brown sugar
2 teaspoons soy sauce
1 garlic clove, minced
1 green bell pepper, cut in squares
3 tablespoons cornstarch
¼ cup water

Place chicken in bottom of a slow cooker. Mix together pineapple syrup, broth, vinegar, brown sugar, and soy sauce in a saucepan. Heat until brown sugar dissolves. Pour over chicken. Heat on high for 1 hour. Add pineapple, garlic, and bell pepper. Cover and cook on low for 7 to 9 hours. Half an hour before serving, mix together cornstarch, and stir into sauce to thicken. Makes 8 servings.

Italian Baked Chicken Breasts

1 cup Italian breadcrumbs
½ cup grated Parmesan cheese
1 teaspoon garlic salt
½ cup butter
1 teaspoon minced garlic
6 boneless, skinless chicken breasts

Combine breadcrumbs, Parmesan cheese, and garlic salt. Melt butter in a small saucepan; add garlic and cook over low heat for 1 minute. Dip chicken breasts in garlic butter, and coat with breadcrumb mixture. Bake on greased baking sheet at 400° for about 20 minutes or until thoroughly cooked. Makes 6 servings.

Italian Chicken and Rice

4 boneless, skinless chicken breasts, cut into wide strips
2 tablespoons olive oil
2 cups chicken broth
1 cup quick-cooking rice
2 teaspoons Italian seasoning
2 teaspoons garlic, minced
Salt and black pepper, to taste

Cook chicken in oil in large skillet until done; add chicken broth, rice,
Italian seasoning, garlic, salt, and pepper. Bring to a boil; reduce heat, cover,
and simmer about 20 minutes. Makes 4 servings.

Italian Chicken and Rice with Vegetables

4 boneless, skinless chicken breasts, cut into wide strips
1 onion, chopped
2 tablespoons olive oil
2 cups chicken broth
1 (14-ounce) can zucchini and tomatoes
1 cup quick-cooking rice
2 teaspoons Italian seasoning
2 teaspoons garlic, minced
Salt and black pepper, to taste

Cook chicken and onion in oil in large skillet until done; add chicken broth,
zucchini and tomatoes, rice, Italian seasoning, garlic, salt, and pepper. Bring
to a boil; reduce heat, cover, and simmer about 20 minutes. Makes 4
servings.

Italian Chicken and Potatoes

1½ pounds boneless, skinless chicken breasts
½ cup zesty Italian salad dressing
⅛ teaspoon black pepper
4 garlic cloves, minced
4 potatoes, cubed

Combine all ingredients in a slow cooker. Cover and cook on low for 6 to 8 hours, until chicken is thoroughly cooked and potatoes are tender. Makes 4 servings.

Italian Chicken and Spaghetti

4 boneless, skinless chicken breasts
1 (14½-ounce) can Italian stewed tomatoes
1 (4-ounce) can mushroom stems and pieces, drained
½ teaspoon dried basil
¼ teaspoon garlic powder
1 tablespoon cornstarch
⅓ cup cold water
Cooked spaghetti

In a large skillet coated with nonstick cooking spray, cook chicken for 5 to 6 minutes on each side, or until the juices run clear. Meanwhile, in a saucepan over medium heat, bring tomatoes, mushrooms, basil, and garlic powder to a boil. Combine cornstarch and water; add to tomato mixture. Return to a boil; cook and stir for 2 minutes. Serve chicken over spaghetti, topped with tomato sauce. Makes 4 servings.

Kona Chicken

1 (3-pound) chicken, cut into pieces
½ cup green onions, chopped
½ cup soy sauce
¼ cup chicken broth
½ cup water
½ cup honey

Place chicken in a slow cooker. Mix together onions, soy sauce, chicken broth, and water. Pour over top of chicken. Cover and cook on low until chicken is tender, 6 to 8 hours. Remove chicken from slow cooker. Brush with honey and place in broiler. Broil until golden brown, brushing with honey several times. Serve with sauce from slow cooker. Makes 8 servings.

Kung Pao Chicken

1 egg white
1 tablespoon plus 1 teaspoon cornstarch, divided
1 teaspoon soy sauce
½ teaspoon salt
Dash white pepper
4 boneless, skinless chicken breasts, cut into ¾-inch pieces
2 tablespoons cold water
½ teaspoon sugar
¼ sesame oil
2 tablespoons vegetable oil
1 medium onion, cut into 8 pieces
1 garlic clove, crushed
1 teaspoon finely chopped ginger
2 tablespoons hoisin sauce
2 teaspoons chile paste
1 large green bell pepper, cut into ¾-inch pieces
½ cup chicken broth
½ cup roasted peanuts
Cooked rice

Mix egg white, 1 teaspoon cornstarch, soy sauce, salt, and white pepper in medium glass or plastic bowl; stir in chicken. Cover and refrigerate 30 minutes. Combine 1 tablespoon cornstarch, water, sugar, and sesame oil, and set aside.

Heat wok until very hot. Add vegetable oil and rotate wok to coat side. Add onion, garlic, and ginger, and stir-fry about 1 minute, or until onion is light brown. Add chicken, stir fry until chicken turns white. Add hoisin sauce and chile paste, cook and stir 30 seconds. Stir in broth, heat to boiling. Stir in cornstarch mixture; cook and stir until thickened. Add bell pepper; cook and stir 30 seconds. Sprinkle with peanuts. Serve over rice. Makes 4 servings.

Lacquered Chicken

1 tablespoon vegetable oil
1 (2-pound) whole chicken
3 very large onions, peeled and chopped
5 large tomatoes, chopped
1 medium orange, unpeeled, seeded, chopped
1 teaspoon sugar
1 teaspoon salt
⅛ teaspoon black pepper
½ cup water
1 bouillon cube, crumbled
3 tablespoons red currant, raspberry, or red grape jelly
¼ cup apple cider

Heat oil in a skillet, and sauté chicken on all sides, turning often. Remove and set aside. Sauté onion in skillet until well browned. Place onions in the bottom of a slow cooker. Add tomatoes, orange, sugar, salt, and pepper in the pot, and set chicken on top. Add water and bouillon cube. Cover and cook on low for 5 to 7 hours.

Before serving, remove the chicken to a deep serving dish and keep warm. Place the vegetables from the slow cooker into a skillet, and simmer until thick. Stir in the jelly and the apple cider, and cook, stirring until the sauce boils. Pour sauce over the chicken. Makes 4 servings.

Lemon Chicken

2 boneless, skinless chicken breasts
½ lemon
Salt and black pepper, to taste

Place chicken in a small slow cooker. Squeeze lemon juice over the chicken. Sprinkle with salt and pepper. Cover and cook on low for 6 to 8 hours. Add more lemon juice if needed. Makes 2 servings.

Lemon Chicken and Rice

1 pound boneless, skinless chicken breasts, cut into strips
1 medium onion, chopped
1 large carrot, thinly sliced
2 garlic cloves, minced
2 tablespoons reduced-calorie margarine
2 tablespoons cornstarch
1 (14½-ounce) can low-sodium chicken broth
2 tablespoons fresh lemon juice
½ teaspoon salt (optional)
1½ cups instant rice
1 cup frozen green peas, thawed

In a skillet, cook first 4 ingredients in margarine for 5 to 7 minutes, or until chicken is no longer pink. In a bowl, combine cornstarch, broth, lemon juice, and salt until smooth. Add to skillet and bring to a boil. Cook and stir for 2 minutes, or until thickened. Add rice and peas. Remove from the heat; cover and let stand for 5 minutes. Makes 4 servings.

Lemon Chicken Stir-Fry

½ cup vegetable stock or water
¼ cup fresh lemon juice
1 tablespoon cornstarch
2 teaspoons apple juice
2 teaspoons low-sodium soy sauce
1 teaspoon chili sauce
1 chicken-flavored bouillon cube, or 1 teaspoon instant chicken bouillon
    granules
2 tablespoons vegetable oil
1 pound boneless, skinless chicken breasts, cut into strips
2 garlic cloves, crushed
4 cups sliced fresh vegetables, such as green onions, fresh mushrooms,
    carrots, red pepper, broccoli florets, snow peas, and celery
2 tablespoons sugar
Cooked rice

For lemon sauce, combine vegetable stock, lemon juice, cornstarch, apple juice, soy sauce, chili sauce, and bouillon in small bowl until smooth. Set aside. Heat oil in wok or frying pan over medium heat. Cook and stir chicken and garlic, until chicken is no longer pink, about 10 minutes. Remove from pan; keep warm.

Add vegetables. Cook and stir about 3 minutes, or until heated through. Return chicken to pan; add lemon sauce and cook until thickened and bubbling. Stir in sugar. Serve over rice. Makes 4 servings.

Lemon Pepper Chicken

1 cup breadcrumbs
2 tablespoons chopped fresh parsley
1 tablespoon lemon zest
1 teaspoon black pepper
½ teaspoon salt
1¼ pounds boneless, skinless chicken breasts
¼ cup plain yogurt

Rinse chicken fillets and pat dry. Combine breadcrumbs with parsley, lemon zest, pepper, and salt. Brush chicken with yogurt, and coat with breadcrumbs. Place on a nonstick baking sheet. Bake at 375° for 20 minutes or until tender. Makes 4 to 5 servings.

Lemon Pepper Chicken #2

4 boneless, skinless chicken breasts
½ lemon
1 teaspoon black pepper

Place chicken in a slow cooker. Squeeze lemon juice over the chicken. Sprinkle with pepper. Cover and cook on low for 6 to 8 hours. Add more lemon juice if needed. Makes 4 servings.

Lemon Rosemary Chicken

Juice of 4 large lemons
1 onion, sliced
1 cup teriyaki sauce
1 cup chicken broth
¼ cup chopped fresh rosemary
1 tablespoon Dijon mustard
2 teaspoons minced garlic
8 boneless, skinless chicken breasts

Combine lemon juice, onion, teriyaki sauce, chicken broth, rosemary, Dijon mustard, and garlic. Lay chicken breasts in a single layer in a large baking dish or roasting pan. Pour lemon juice mixture over chicken, turning to coat. Bake at 400° for about 20 minutes or until cooked through. Makes 8 servings.

Lime Chicken

4 boneless, skinless chicken breasts
¼ cup lime juice
2 tablespoons olive oil
½ teaspoon dried oregano
½ teaspoon garlic salt

Combine all ingredients in a slow cooker. Cover and cook on low for 8 hours. Add liquid if necessary. Makes 4 servings.

Linguine with Chicken Scampi

1 cup breadcrumbs
1½ teaspoons salt, divided
¾ teaspoon pepper, divided
4 boneless, skinless chicken breasts, cut into ½-inch pieces
1 egg, beaten
2 tablespoons olive oil
¼ cup plus 2 tablespoons butter, divided
3 cloves garlic, minced
1 tablespoon lemon juice
16 ounces linguine, cooked according to package directions
½ cup chopped fresh parsley
Lemon wedges

Combine breadcrumbs, 1 teaspoon salt, and ¼ teaspoon pepper. Dip chicken in egg, and dredge in breadcrumbs. Warm the olive oil in a skillet over medium heat. Sauté chicken until breadcrumbs are golden brown. Remove chicken to warm platter. Wipe out skillet with paper towel. Melt ¼ cup butter in skillet. Add garlic, lemon juice, ½ teaspoon salt, and ½ teaspoon pepper; mix well. Turn chicken in sauce to coat. Toss linguine with 2 tablespoons butter, and spoon chicken and sauce over top. Sprinkle with parsley. Garnish with lemon wedges. Makes 4 servings.

Marinated Grilled Chicken

⅓ cup fresh lemon juice
¼ cup water
½ teaspoon garlic powder
¼ teaspoon onion powder
1 teaspoon dried parsley
¼ teaspoon salt
4 boneless, skinless chicken breasts

Mix first 6 ingredients together. Pour mixture over chicken, and marinate in the refrigerator for 2 hours or overnight. Grill over a slow charcoal grill or gas grill on low, turning and basting occasionally until done. Put reserved marinade into a saucepan, bring to a boil, and simmer for 5 minutes. Serve on the side as a sauce. Makes 4 servings.

Mexican Chicken Casserole

2 boneless, skinless chicken breasts, cut into 1-inch cubes
1 teaspoon canola oil
1 small onion, chopped
½ medium green bell pepper, chopped
1 teaspoon chopped garlic
1 cup salsa
½ cup low-fat sour cream, divided
1 cup crushed unsalted, low-fat tortilla chips

Heat oil in large skillet over medium-high heat. Add chicken, onion, bell pepper, and garlic. Cook and stir for 5 to 10 minutes. Remove from heat. Combine ½ cup salsa and ¼ cup sour cream in small bowl until blended. Stir salsa mixture into chicken mixture. Coat a glass casserole dish with cooking spray. Sprinkle ½ cup crushed chips into prepared casserole dish. Spread chicken mixture over crushed chips. Top with remaining crushed chips, and then with remaining salsa. Bake at 325° for 30 minutes, or until heated through. Let stand for 5 minutes before serving. Top each serving with a dollop of remaining sour cream. Makes 2 servings.

Mint Cilantro Chicken Curry

2 cups chopped cilantro
½ cup chopped mint
2 jalapeños, finely chopped
1½ cups chopped red onion
1 tablespoon minced ginger
1 cup water
½ cup canola oil
1½ tablespoons cumin seeds
1 tablespoon coriander seed
3 tablespoons crushed garlic
1 tablespoon salt
2 cups plain yogurt, divided
3 pounds chicken thighs with bone
3 cups cooked basmati rice

Combine cilantro, mint, jalapenõs, onion, ginger, and water in a food processor. Purée until smooth and set aside.

Heat oil in a heavy shallow pot on medium heat for 1 minute. Add cumin and coriander seeds, and allow them to sizzle for about 30 seconds. Add garlic and sauté for about 3 minutes until golden brown. Stir in salt.

Turn off the heat and after 2 to 3 minutes, stir in 1 cup yogurt. Add chicken thighs and stir well. Turn the heat to medium, cover, and cook for about 25 minutes, stirring regularly. Remove curry from the heat and cool for about 20 minutes. Transfer chicken to a mixing bowl and remove meat from bone. Stir in mint cilantro chutney and the remaining cup of yogurt. About 15 minutes before serving, bring curry to a boil on medium heat. Reduce heat and simmer uncovered for about 10 more minutes. Serve over rice. Makes 8 servings.

Moo Goo Gai Pan

1 egg white, lightly beaten
1 tablespoon cornstarch
1 tablespoon rice vinegar
1 teaspoon salt, divided
½ teaspoon white pepper
4 boneless, skinless chicken breasts, sliced into ¼-inch strips
4 tablespoons vegetable oil, divided
½ pound small fresh mushrooms
2½ cups thinly sliced celery
1 (8½-ounce) can water chestnuts, drained and thinly sliced
1 (6-ounce) package frozen snow peas
½ cup sliced green onion
½ teaspoon finely minced garlic
2 teaspoons soy sauce
1 teaspoon sugar
Cooked rice

In a small bowl, combine egg white, cornstarch, vinegar, ¼ teaspoon of salt, and white pepper; blend well. Add chicken, coating well. In a wok or large skillet, heat 2 tablespoons vegetable oil. Add mushrooms, celery, water chestnuts, snow peas, and remaining salt; sauté 5 minutes. Remove vegetables from wok; reserve. Heat remaining 2 tablespoons oil in wok. Add green onion, garlic, and chicken; cook over high heat. Stir constantly. Stir in soy sauce, sugar, and vegetable mixture; cook 2 minutes longer. Stir often. Remove to a heated platter. Serve at once over rice. Makes 4 servings.

Onion and Mushroom Chicken

1 (2½- to 3-pound) whole chicken, cut into pieces
1 (1-ounce) package onion mushroom soup mix
½ teaspoon salt
¼ teaspoon dried thyme
1 garlic clove, minced
1½ cups beef broth
½ cup water
1 can small onions, drained
2 tablespoons chopped fresh parsley

Place the chicken in a slow cooker. Mix together all remaining ingredients and pour over chicken. Cover and cook on low for 8 hours. Makes 6 servings.

Orange Chicken

½ teaspoon salt
½ teaspoon chili powder
½ teaspoon cayenne pepper
½ teaspoon paprika
4 boneless, skinless chicken breasts
1 cup onion, chopped
½ cup chopped bell pepper
½ cup chopped celery
2 garlic cloves, minced
¾ cup orange juice
1 teaspoon grated orange peel
2 tablespoons honey
1 tablespoon Worcestershire sauce
½ teaspoon ground ginger

Combine salt, chile powder, cayenne pepper, and paprika. Sprinkle over chicken. Set aside. Place onion, bell pepper, celery, and garlic in the bottom of a slow cooker. Place chicken on top. Mix orange juice, peel, honey, Worcestershire sauce, and ginger. Pour over chicken. Cover and cook on low for 6 to 8 hours. Makes 4 servings.

Orange-Glazed Chicken

½ cup orange marmalade
⅓ cup Russian dressing
½ (1-ounce) package dry onion soup mix
6 frozen chicken breasts, unthawed

Mix the first 3 ingredients together. Place chicken in slow cooker, and cover with marmalade mixture. Cover and cook on low 6 to 8 hours. Makes 6 servings.

Orzo Pasta with Chicken and Broccoli

2¼ cups chicken broth
2 large boneless, skinless chicken breasts, cut into chunks
4 cups broccoli florets
6 ounces orzo pasta, cooked and drained
2 tablespoons olive oil
2 tablespoons vinegar
1 tablespoon Dijon mustard
1 teaspoon parsley flakes
½ teaspoon minced garlic
Salt and black pepper, to taste

Bring chicken broth to boil in a large saucepan. Add chicken and return to a boil. Reduce heat; cover and simmer for 5 minutes. Add broccoli and cook an additional 3 to 5 minutes, or until broccoli is crisp and tender and chicken is cooked through.

Drain chicken and broccoli. Toss with orzo and remaining ingredients. Makes 4 servings.

Oven-Fried Chicken

6 to 8 pieces chicken, on the bone
½ cup all-purpose flour
1 teaspoon salt
¼ teaspoon black pepper
½ teaspoon paprika
½ cup margarine, melted

Coat chicken with mixture of flour, salt, pepper, and paprika. Pour melted margarine in a baking pan. Dip chicken pieces in margarine; arrange on baking sheets. Bake at 400° for 30 minutes; turn. Bake for 25 minutes, or until chicken is tender. Makes 8 servings.

Oven-Fried Chicken #2

1½ cups nonfat dry milk
1 tablespoon paprika
2 teaspoons poultry seasoning
¼ teaspoon black pepper
4 boneless, skinless chicken breasts

Combine first 4 ingredients in a large resealable plastic bag. Add chicken, one piece at a time, and shake to coat. Place in an 8-inch-square baking pan that has been coated with nonstick cooking spray. Bake uncovered at 350° for 30 minutes, or until juices run clear. Bake for 1 hour, or until meat thermometer reads 160° to 170°. Makes 4 servings.

Oven-Fried Chicken Fingers

1 cup low-fat mayonnaise
1 tablespoon curry paste
Water
Salt and black pepper, to taste
4 boneless, skinless chicken breasts, cut into thick strips
2 cups breadcrumbs

In a large bowl, combine the mayonnaise and curry paste. Thin this with a little water, 1 tablespoon at a time, until you get the consistency of heavy cream; season with salt and pepper.

Drop the strips into the bowl and coat them well with the curry mayonnaise. Cover and refrigerate for at least 5 minutes or up to 1 hour. Pour the breadcrumbs onto a plate and toss the chicken strips well to completely cover them. Put them onto a nonstick baking sheet and into the oven. Bake at 350° for 15 to 20 minutes, or until the chicken is browned and cooked through. Makes 4 servings.

Oven-Fried Pecan Chicken

½ **cup butter**
1 cup all-purpose flour
1 teaspoon baking powder
2 teaspoons garlic salt
2 teaspoons paprika
½ **teaspoon black pepper**
½ **cup pecans, chopped**
1 tablespoon sesame seeds
1 egg, beaten
½ **cup milk**
6 boneless, skinless chicken breasts

Melt butter in large glass baking dish at 375°; set aside. Combine flour, baking powder, garlic salt, paprika, pepper, pecans, and sesame seeds in a large shallow dish. Combine egg and milk in a separate dish. Dip each chicken breast in egg mixture, and then dredge in flour mixture. Place in melted butter, and bake about 25 minutes or until cooked through. Makes 6 servings.

Paprika Chicken

⅓ cup plus 2 tablespoons all-purpose flour
1 tablespoon paprika
½ teaspoon salt
⅛ teaspoon black pepper
4 boneless, skinless chicken breasts (about 4 ounces each)
1 large onion, chopped
2½ cups nonfat low-sodium chicken broth
1 chicken bouillon cube, dissolved in ½ cup hot water
½ cup low-fat sour cream

In large bowl, mix ⅓ cup flour, paprika, salt, and pepper. Spray large skillet well with cooking spray. Dredge chicken breasts in flour mixture, and brown on both sides in skillet over medium-high heat. Cover chicken breasts with chopped onion. Pour 1 cup chicken broth and the bouillon over chicken and onions. Cover skillet and reduce heat to low. Simmer until chicken is done, 20 to 30 minutes.

Remove chicken and onions from skillet, and keep warm. Combine remaining 1½ cups broth and 2 tablespoons flour. Add to liquid in skillet, bring to a boil, whisking continuously. Lower heat and continue whisking until thickened, about 5 minutes. Pour over chicken and onions. Makes 4 servings.

Paella à la Valenciana

2 cups chicken broth
3 sprigs fresh rosemary
Salt
¼ teaspoon crumbled saffron
4 cups water
8 tablespoons olive oil
3 pounds chicken, cut into pieces
1 green bell pepper, finely chopped
1 medium onion, finely chopped
8 garlic cloves, minced
8 ounces green beans
8 ounces snap peas, strings removed
1 package frozen artichoke hearts
2 medium tomatoes, finely chopped
2 tablespoons minced flat-leaf parsley
1 teaspoon paprika
3 cups quick-cooking rice
1 pimento, sliced lengthwise into ¼-inch strips

Heat broth, rosemary, salt, saffron, and 4 cups water in a covered pot over the lowest heat for 20 minutes. Remove the rosemary.

Heat oil over medium-high heat in a large pan. Sauté chicken until brown, about 5 minutes, turning once. Add the green pepper, onion, and garlic, and cook until slightly softened. Stir in the green beans, peas, and artichokes, and cook on high for about 3 minutes. Add the tomatoes and parsley, cook 1 minute, then mix in the paprika.

Stir in rice and coat well with the pan mixture. Pour in the hot broth and bring to a boil. Boil about 5 minutes, stirring occasionally.

Arrange the pimento strips over rice in a wagon wheel pattern, and transfer pan to the oven. Cook, uncovered, at 400° until rice is almost done, about 10 to 15 minutes. Remove to a warm spot, cover with foil, and let sit 5 to 10 minutes, until rice is cooked to taste. Makes 8 servings.

Peachy Chicken

4 boneless, skinless chicken thighs
2 sweet potatoes, peeled and cubed
1 onion, chopped
2 tablespoons water
3 tablespoons cornstarch
½ cup peach preserves

Put chicken in a slow cooker, and top with sweet potatoes and onions. Cover and cook on low for 7 to 8 hours, until chicken is thoroughly cooked and sweet potatoes are tender when pierced with fork. Remove chicken, sweet potatoes, and onions from slow cooker with a slotted spoon, and cover with foil to keep warm.

In a heavy saucepan, combine water and cornstarch, and mix well. Add juices from slow cooker along with preserves. Cook and stir over medium heat, stirring frequently, until mixture boils and thickens. Cook for 2 minutes, and pour over chicken and vegetables. Makes 4 servings.

Peanut Chicken

3½ pounds boneless, skinless chicken breasts
⅓ cup peanut butter
2 tablespoons low-sodium soy sauce
3 tablespoons orange juice
⅛ teaspoon black pepper
4 cups cooked rice or noodles

Combine all ingredients in a slow cooker; mix well. Cover and cook on low for 6 to 8 hours, or until chicken is tender and thoroughly cooked. Serve with rice or noodles. Makes 8 servings.

Pecan Crusted Chicken Breasts

1 cup all-purpose flour
1½ cups chopped pecans
1 tablespoon oregano
2 teaspoons ground cumin
1 teaspoon chili powder
1 teaspoon dried thyme
½ teaspoon cayenne pepper
4 boneless, skinless chicken breasts, pounded to ¼-inch thickness
¾ cup butter

Combine flour, pecans, oregano, cumin, chili powder, thyme, and cayenne. In a large frying pan, melt butter. Dip chicken breasts in butter, and then roll in the flour mixture. Increase heat, and cook chicken for about 5 minutes for each side. Drain on paper towels. Makes 4 servings.

Peking Chicken Pizza

½ pound boneless, skinless chicken breasts, pounded to ¼-inch thickness
Extra-virgin olive oil, for drizzling
Poultry seasoning
2 tablespoons all-purpose flour
1 package refrigerated pizza dough
2 to 3 tablespoons sesame seeds
3 tablespoons plum sauce or Peking duck sauce
3 tablespoons barbecue sauce
2 cups shredded Monterey Jack cheese
2 scallions, chopped in 1-inch pieces on an angle
¼ red bell pepper, chopped

Heat a grill pan over high heat. Drizzle oil over chicken cutlets, and season. Grill chicken 3 or 4 minutes on each side. Slice chicken into very thin strips.

Sprinkle a pizza pan or baking stone with flour. Press out dough, working all the way to edges of the pan. Sprinkle the edges of your dough with sesame seeds. Cover the pie with plum sauce or duck sauce and barbecue sauce. Cover pie with cheese. Top with sliced chicken, scallions, and red bell pepper. Bake at 450° for 12 to 15 minutes, until crisp and bubbly. Makes 8 servings.

Picnic Drumsticks

1 cup crushed saltine crackers
2 tablespoons dry onion soup mix
8 chicken legs
⅓ cup butter, melted

Stir together crackers and onion soup mix. Dip chicken legs into melted butter, and then coat with cracker mixture. Place remaining butter in a baking pan, and then top with coated chicken legs. Sprinkle with any remaining crumb mixture.

Bake at 350° for 45 to 55 minutes, or until chicken is tender and thoroughly cooked. Makes 8 servings.

Pineapple Honey Chicken

4 boneless, skinless chicken breasts
2 teaspoons flour
½ cup butter
¼ cup honey
⅓ cup brown sugar
Garlic salt, to taste
1 cup pineapple juice
1 (15-ounce) can pineapple chunks, drained

Coat chicken in flour. In a large skillet, melt butter and brown chicken. Remove chicken and add honey, brown sugar, garlic salt, and pineapple juice to the skillet. Stir until thickened. Arrange chicken in baking dish with pineapple chunks, and pour sauce on top. Bake for 45 minutes at 350°. Makes 4 servings.

Pineapple Tarragon Chicken

1 (6-ounce) can frozen pineapple juice concentrate, thawed
¼ cup honey
1 teaspoon dried tarragon
Salt and black pepper, to taste
6 chicken breasts, on the bone

Prepare and heat grill, placing coals to one side for indirect cooking. Make aluminum foil drip pan, and place opposite coals under grill rack. In small saucepan, combine juice concentrate, honey, tarragon, salt, and pepper. Cook over medium heat for 3 to 5 minutes until blended.

Place chicken breasts on grill over drip pan. Baste with sauce. Grill, turning and basting frequently with sauce, until chicken is thoroughly cooked, about 25 to 35 minutes. Cook any remaining sauce over medium heat until boiling. Boil for 2 minutes, stirring frequently. Serve with chicken. Makes 6 servings.

Pizza Chicken

8 boneless, skinless chicken breasts
¼ teaspoon salt
⅛ teaspoon black pepper
1 onion, chopped
2 bell peppers, cut into 1-inch pieces
2 cups pasta sauce
1 cup shredded Mozzarella cheese
Cooked pasta or rice

Sprinkle chicken with salt and pepper and place in a slow cooker. Top with onions and bell peppers and pour pasta sauce over all. Cover and cook on low for 4 to 5 hours, until chicken is thoroughly cooked. Stir well, then sprinkle with cheese and let stand 5 minutes to melt. Serve over cooked pasta or rice. Makes 8 servings.

Potato Chip Chicken

½ cup mayonnaise
2 tablespoons Dijon mustard
2 tablespoons milk
1 teaspoon Italian seasoning
1 teaspoon garlic salt
Black pepper, to taste
6 boneless, skinless chicken breasts
2 cups crushed potato chips

Combine mayonnaise, Dijon mustard, milk, Italian seasoning, garlic salt, and pepper to taste. Dip chicken breasts in mayonnaise mixture, and then roll in potato chip crumbs. Bake on a greased baking sheet at 400° for about 30 minutes. Makes 6 servings.

Quick and Tasty Chicken

1 (10¾-ounce) can cream of chicken soup
1 (8-ounce) box Velveeta cheese
4 pieces baked chicken

In a small saucepan, heat soup. Add cheese. Keep on low heat until well blended. Spoon over baked chicken. Makes 4 servings.

Quick Arroz con Pollo

3 cups cooked rice
3 cups cooked and chopped chicken
1 (10¾-ounce) can nacho cheese soup
1 (10-ounce) can diced tomatoes with chiles, drained
2 cups shredded Monterey Jack cheese, divided

Combine rice, chicken, soup, tomatoes, and 1 cup cheese. Pour into large greased baking dish. Sprinkle remaining cup of cheese over top. Bake at 350° for about 40 minutes. Makes 6 servings.

Quick Oriental Cashew Chicken

1½ cups microwave spiral pasta, uncooked
1 (14-ounce) can chicken chow mein
1 cup chicken broth
½ cup cashews

In a 2-quart microwave-safe casserole, stir together pasta, chow mein, and broth. Cover; microwave on high for 8 to 10 minutes, stirring once, or until pasta is tender. Stir in cashews. Makes 2 servings.

Roasted Chicken

1 (3- to 4-pound) whole chicken
3 tablespoons butter
3 garlic cloves, minced
1 teaspoon salt
1 tablespoon black pepper
3 sprigs rosemary
3 sprigs thyme
1 lemon, quartered

Rub entire chicken with mixture of butter, garlic, salt, and pepper. Place rosemary and thyme sprigs along with lemon inside cavity. Tie legs together with butcher's string if necessary. Place on a lightly greased roasting pan. Bake at 450° for 30 minutes. Reduce heat to 350°; bake for 1 hour or until done. Makes 6 to 8 servings.

Roasted Chicken with Sage Dressing

2 cups unseasoned dry breadcrumbs
½ cup chopped onion
¼ cup chopped fresh parsley
3 tablespoons chopped fresh sage
Egg substitute equal to 1 egg
¾ cup low-sodium chicken broth
1 (3- to 4-pound) roasting chicken

In a large bowl, combine breadcrumbs, onion, parsley, sage, and egg. Add enough broth to moisten. Stuff loosely into chicken. Fasten with skewers to close. Place with breast side up on a shallow rack in roasting pan. Brush with butter, if desired. Bake uncovered at 375° for about 2 hours, or until juices run clear. Baste several times with pan juices. Makes 6 to 8 servings.

Saucy Chicken

6 boneless, skinless chicken breasts
2 cups salsa
⅓ cup brown sugar
2 tablespoon honey Dijon mustard

Combine all ingredients and place in a baking dish. Bake at 350° for 40 to 45 minutes, until chicken is thoroughly cooked. Makes 6 servings.

Savory Italian Wings

1½ cups cracker crumbs
1 cup grated Parmesan cheese
1 (0.7-ounce) package Italian dressing mix
2 pounds chicken wings
½ cup butter, melted

Combine crumbs, cheese, and Italian dressing mix. Coat wings with melted butter, and then crumb mixture. Bake on greased baking sheet at 350° for about 30 minutes. Makes about 6 servings.

Sesame Chicken

3 boneless, skinless chicken breasts, cut into cubes
4 tablespoons soy sauce, divided
¼ cup plus 1 tablespoon rice vinegar, divided
2 tablespoons plus 1 teaspoon sesame oil, divided
2 tablespoons all-purpose flour
¼ cup plus 2 tablespoons cornstarch, divided
½ cup plus 2 tablespoons water, divided
¼ teaspoon baking powder
¼ teaspoon baking soda
1 teaspoon vegetable oil
1 cup chicken broth
1 cup sugar
1 teaspoon chile paste
1 garlic clove, minced
4 cups peanut oil
2 tablespoons toasted sesame seeds
Cooked rice

Combine 2 tablespoons soy sauce, 1 tablespoon rice vinegar, 1 teaspoon sesame oil, flour, 2 tablespoons cornstarch, 2 tablespoons water, baking powder, baking soda, and vegetable oil. Place chicken in mixture, and marinate for 20 to 30 minutes.

In a saucepan, combine ½ cup water, chicken broth, ¼ cup rice vinegar, ¼ cup cornstarch, sugar, 2 tablespoons soy sauce, chile paste, and garlic. Turn heat to high and bring to a boil. Turn heat to low, and let simmer until ready to serve.

In a large frying pan, warm the peanut oil over medium high heat. Fry chicken in batches, and drain on paper towels. Place the chicken on a large platter, and pour the sauce over. Sprinkle with sesame seeds, and serve with rice. Makes 8 servings.

Sesame Chicken Strips

1 cup sour cream
1 tablespoon lemon juice
2 teaspoons celery salt
2 teaspoons Worcestershire sauce
½ teaspoon salt
¼ teaspoon black pepper
2 garlic cloves, minced
6 boneless, skinless chicken breasts, cut crosswise into ½-inch strips
1 cup dry breadcrumbs
⅓ cup sesame seeds
4 tablespoons butter, melted

In a large bowl, combine sour cream, lemon juice, celery salt, Worcestershire sauce, salt, pepper, and garlic. Mix well. Add chicken to mixture, coat well, and cover. Refrigerate at least 8 hours or overnight.

In medium bowl, combine breadcrumbs and sesame seeds. Remove chicken strips from sour cream mixture. Roll in crumb mixture, coating evenly. Arrange in single layer in greased pan. Spoon butter evenly over chicken. Bake at 350° for 18 to 25 minutes, or until chicken is tender and golden brown. Makes 6 servings.

Sesame Mushroom Chicken

1 (10¾-ounce) can golden mushroom soup
¾ cup milk
2 tablespoons butter, melted
2 cups cracker crumbs
¼ cup sesame seeds
6 boneless, skinless chicken breasts

Combine soup, milk, and butter. Combine cracker crumbs and sesame seeds. Dip chicken breasts in soup mixture, and coat with cracker crumb mixture. Place in large greased baking dish, and pour remaining soup mixture over chicken. Bake at 400° for about 45 minutes. Makes 6 servings.

Slow Cooker Sweet-and-Sour Chicken

2 pounds boneless, skinless chicken thighs, cut into 1½-inch pieces
1 (26-ounce) jar sweet-and-sour simmer sauce
1 (16-ounce) package frozen broccoli, carrots, and peppers, thawed and drained

Mix chicken with simmer sauce in slow cooker. Cover and cook on low for 8 to 10 hours, or until chicken is tender and no longer pink. Right before serving, stir in vegetables. Cover, increase heat to high, and cook for 10 to 15 minutes, or until vegetables are crisp and tender. Makes 4 to 6 servings.

Smothered Chicken and Vegetables

3 carrots, sliced
3 celery stalks, sliced
1 large onion, cut into thin wedges
3 cups cooked and cubed chicken
1 (10¾-ounce) can cream of celery soup
¾ cup chicken broth

Place vegetables in bottom of a slow cooker. Top with chicken. Add soup and broth. Cover and cook for 4 to 6 hours on low. Makes 3 to 4 servings.

Sour Cream and Bacon Chicken

8 bacon slices
8 boneless, skinless chicken breasts
2 (10¾-ounce) cans cream of mushroom soup with roasted garlic
1 cup sour cream
½ cup all-purpose flour

Wrap one slice of bacon around each boneless chicken breast, and place in a slow cooker. In medium bowl, combine condensed soups, sour cream, and flour, and mix with wire whisk to blend. Pour over chicken. Cover and cook on low for 6 to 8 hours until chicken and bacon are thoroughly cooked. Makes 8 servings.

Southern Baked Chicken

1 teaspoon chili powder
1 teaspoon paprika
¼ teaspoon garlic powder
¼ teaspoon salt
¼ teaspoon pepper
⅔ cup self-rising cornmeal
1 (2½- to 3-pound) chicken, cut into pieces
¼ cup milk
¼ cup butter, melted

Combine the chili powder, paprika, garlic powder, salt, pepper, and cornmeal. Dip pieces of chicken in the milk, and dredge in cornmeal mixture. Place chicken, skin-side up, on a greased baking dish. Lightly brush with melted butter. Bake at 375° for 50 to 55 minutes, or until juices run clear when chicken is pierced by a fork. Makes 4 servings.

Southern Fried Chicken

1 (3- to 4-pound) chicken, cut into pieces
1 teaspoon salt
1 teaspoon black pepper
2 cups buttermilk
2 cups all-purpose flour
1 teaspoon garlic powder
1 teaspoon paprika
Vegetable oil

Season chicken with salt and pepper. In a large dish, pour buttermilk over chicken. Allow to soak for 2 hours in refrigerator. Combine flour, garlic powder, and paprika. Dredge chicken in flour mixture, and fry, a few pieces at a time, in preheated oil until golden brown, 8 to 10 minutes for white meat and 12 to 14 minutes for dark meat. Remove from oil and drain. Makes 6 to 8 servings.

South of the Border Chicken

4 boneless, skinless chicken breasts
1 (10¾-ounce) can broccoli cheese soup
⅓ cup evaporated milk
4 cups cooked rice
Salsa
Sour cream
1 small avocado, sliced (optional)

Place chicken in bottom of a slow cooker and cover with soup and milk. Cover and cook on low for 7 to 8 hours. Serve with rice. Top with salsa, sour cream, and avocado. Makes 4 servings.

Southwestern Chicken and Lentil Burritos

2 cups dried lentils
4 cups water
4 cups cooked and chopped chicken
1 (14-ounce) can Mexican-style corn, drained
1 (10-ounce) can diced tomatoes with chiles
1 onion, chopped
1 (6-ounce) can tomato paste
½ cup bulgur wheat
2 tablespoons chili powder
1 tablespoon minced garlic
2 teaspoons dried oregano
Salt and black pepper, to taste
1 tablespoon vinegar
12 (10-inch) flour tortillas
2 cups shredded Cheddar cheese

Combine all ingredients except vinegar, tortillas, and cheese; bring to a boil. Reduce heat, cover, and simmer for about 1½ hours. Stir in vinegar. Serve in flour tortillas with cheese. Makes 12 servings.

Soy Chicken

½ cup vinegar
6 to 8 garlic cloves, crushed
½ teaspoon black peppercorns
1 bay leaf
½ tablespoon salt
2½ tablespoons soy sauce
¼ cup water
1 (3- to 4-pound) whole chicken, cut into pieces

In a slow cooker, combine vinegar, garlic, peppercorns, bay leaf, salt, and soy sauce. Add chicken. Cover and cook on high for 1 hour. Add water. Turn heat setting to low, and cook for 4 to 5 hours. Makes 6 to 8 servings.

Spanish Chicken with Mushrooms

1 teaspoon paprika
1 teaspoon garlic powder
Salt and black pepper, to taste
3 pounds chicken breasts, on the bone
1 (6-ounce) can tomato paste
1 cup water
1 (8-ounce) can mushrooms, sliced
3 cups cooked rice

Combine paprika, garlic powder, salt, and pepper. Sprinkle spice mixture on each piece of chicken. Place chicken in a slow cooker. Mix tomato paste and water together. Pour over the chicken. Add sliced mushrooms. Cover and cook on low for 7 to 9 hours. Serve over rice. Makes 6 to 8 servings.

Spanish Chicken with Yellow Rice

2 tablespoons olive oil
2 medium onions, chopped
4 garlic cloves, minced
2 celery stalks, diced
2 medium red or green bell peppers, cut into strips
1 cup chopped mushrooms
2 cups uncooked rice
1 (3-pound) chicken, cut into 8 pieces, skin removed
1 teaspoon salt (optional)
3½ cups low-sodium chicken broth
4 cups water
Dash saffron
3 medium tomatoes, chopped
1 cup frozen green peas
1 cup frozen corn kernels
1 cup frozen green beans
Olives or capers (optional)

Heat oil over medium heat in a nonstick pot. Add onion, garlic, celery, pepper, and mushrooms. Cook, stirring often, for about 3 minutes until tender. Add rice and sauté for 2 to 3 minutes, stirring constantly, until it begins to brown. Add the chicken, salt, chicken broth, water, saffron, and tomatoes. Bring the pot to a boil; reduce heat to medium-low, cover, and let the casserole simmer, until the water is absorbed and rice is tender, about 20 minutes. Stir in the peas, corn, and beans, and cook for 8 to 10 minutes. Garnish with olives or capers, if desired. Makes 6 servings.

Spinach Chicken Rollups

1 (8-ounce) package nonfat cream cheese, softened
3 tablespoons chopped green onion
1½ cups cooked and chopped chicken breast
2 tablespoons nonfat sour cream
1 teaspoon dried dill weed
4 (10-inch) low-fat flour tortillas
1½ cups fresh spinach leaves
Nonfat ranch salad dressing or salsa

Combine cream cheese, onion, chicken, sour cream, and dill in medium bowl; mix until blended. Spread ¼ cup filling on each tortilla; place spinach leaves on top, leaving about ½-inch border. Roll tortillas tightly and wrap in plastic wrap. Refrigerate for at least 1 hour before serving. Slice in half, and serve with nonfat ranch dressing or salsa. Makes 4 servings.

Spice-Crusted Chicken Thighs with Cucumber Lemon Raita

⅓ teaspoon ground cardamom
2½ teaspoons ground coriander
2½ teaspoons ground cumin
2½ teaspoons ground fennel
1½ teaspoons salt, divided
1 teaspoon black pepper, divided
6 boneless, skinless chicken thighs
2 tablespoons extra virgin olive oil, divided
1 cucumber, peeled, seeded, and grated
1 cup plain yogurt
1 tablespoon grated lemon zest
1 garlic clove, minced
⅛ teaspoon cayenne pepper

In a small bowl, combine cardamom, coriander, cumin, fennel, 1 teaspoon salt, and ½ teaspoon black pepper. Mix well. Reserve 1 teaspoon spice mixture, and pour the rest into a large resealable plastic bag. Brush chicken thighs evenly with 1 tablespoon olive oil, and place in bag. Shake to coat chicken with spice mixture. Set aside.

Place cucumber on several layers of paper towels; top with more paper towels. Pat well to remove excess water. In medium bowl, stir together cucumber, yogurt, lemon zest, garlic, cayenne, and reserved spice mixture. Season with remaining ½ teaspoon salt and ½ teaspoon black pepper. Set aside.

Warm the remaining 1 tablespoon olive oil in a large skillet over medium-high heat. Add chicken and cook in single layer until skin is golden brown, about 3 to 5 minutes. Reduce the heat to low, turn chicken, and cook until done, about 4 to 5 minutes longer. Place chicken thighs on serving platter, top with yogurt sauce, and serve immediately. Makes 6 servings.

Spicy Chicken

1 (3-pound) whole chicken
1 medium potato, peeled and sliced
2 onions, finely chopped
4 to 7 garlic cloves, minced
2 bay leaves
1 teaspoon ground cumin
1 teaspoon dried oregano
1 tablespoon chili powder
2 cups soft white breadcrumbs
2 chicken bouillon cubes
1¾ cups water
Chopped fresh cilantro

Place chicken in a slow cooker. Place potato slices around bottom sides of pot. Add onions, garlic, spices, and breadcrumbs, pushing the crumbs down around the chicken. Microwave bouillon cubes with water, and pour over the chicken. Cover and cook on low heat 7 hours or on high heat for 4 hours.

Remove lid and let cool for about 20 minutes. Carefully lift chicken onto a plate using two wide-slotted spoons. Remove and discard bay leaves, skin, and bones. When sauce is still very warm (not hot), use a slotted spoon to check for remaining bones. Then pour sauce into a food processor or blender, and process until smooth. Serve chicken with sauce, and garnish with cilantro. Makes 6 servings.

Stir-Fried Ginger and Scallion Chicken

1 (1-pound) package boneless chicken tenders
½ tablespoon corn flour
3 tablespoons vegetable oil, divided
1 (2-inch) piece fresh ginger, peeled and sliced
4 scallions, cut into 2-inch sections
2 tablespoons oyster sauce
⅛ teaspoon sesame oil
½ tablespoon rice vinegar
¼ teaspoon sugar
Salt and black pepper, to taste

Coat chicken in corn flour and 1 tablespoon of vegetable oil. Marinate for 15 to 20 minutes. Place wok over medium-high heat and add remaining vegetable oil. When the oil begins to smoke, add the ginger and stir for a few seconds. Add the scallions and stir for 30 seconds. Add chicken, oyster sauce, sesame oil, vinegar, sugar, salt, and pepper. Stir-fry until chicken is cooked through. Makes 4 servings.

Sunday Chicken

1 (10¾-ounce) can cream of mushroom soup
1 (10¾-ounce) can cream of celery soup
1 (10¾-ounce) can cream of chicken soup
¼ cup melted butter, divided
1¼ cups quick-cooking rice
1 (3- to 4-pound) chicken, cut into pieces
Salt and black pepper, to taste
Paprika, to taste

In a medium bowl, combine soups, 2 tablespoons butter, and the rice. Pour into a greased dish. Place chicken pieces over rice mixture and brush with remaining butter. Season with salt and pepper. Sprinkle with paprika. Bake at 275° about 2½ hours or until tender. Makes 4 to 6 servings.

Sunshine Chicken

8 skinless, boneless chicken breasts
1 cup barbecue sauce
1 cup orange juice

Place chicken breasts in a slow cooker. Combine barbecue sauce with orange juice. Pour over chicken. Cover and cook on low for 8 hours. Makes 8 servings.

Sweet-and-Sour Chicken

6 boneless, skinless chicken breasts
1 (6-ounce) can frozen orange juice concentrate, thawed
¼ cup soy sauce
1 (1-ounce) package onion soup mix
1 green bell pepper, chopped
1 (8-ounce) can pineapple chunks, drained

Place chicken in a large greased baking dish. Combine orange juice concentrate, soy sauce, and onion soup mix. Toss with bell pepper and pineapple, and pour over chicken, turning to coat. Bake at 400° for 20 to 30 minutes. Makes 6 servings.

Sweet-and-Sour Chicken #2

1 cup low-sodium chicken broth
1 tablespoon low-sodium soy sauce
1 tablespoon cornstarch
2 tablespoons brown sugar
2 tablespoons rice vinegar
½ teaspoon ground ginger
1 tablespoon cooking oil
1 pound boneless, skinless chicken breasts, cut into 1-inch pieces
1 cup chopped green bell pepper
1 cup sliced carrot
½ cup chopped onion
1 garlic clove, minced
1 (8-ounce) can unsweetened pineapple chunks, drained
Cooked rice

Combine first 6 ingredients; stir well. Heat oil in a large nonstick skillet over medium-high heat. Add chicken and stir-fry for 5 minutes. Add green pepper, carrots, onion, and garlic, and stir-fry for 2 minutes. Add broth mixture and pineapple to skillet, bring to a boil, and cook for 1 minute, stirring constantly. Serve over rice. Makes 4 servings.

Swiss Mushroom Chicken

6 boneless, skinless chicken breasts, pounded to ¼-inch thickness
6 pieces Swiss cheese
1 (10¾-ounce) can cream of mushroom soup with roasted garlic
3 tablespoons water
¼ teaspoon black pepper

Place a piece of cheese in the center of each chicken breast. Fold up and
secure with toothpicks. Place in a slow cooker. Combine remaining
ingredients, and pour over chicken bundles, making sure pieces are fully
covered. Cover and cook on low for 6 to 7 hours, until chicken is thoroughly
cooked. Makes 6 servings.

Tangy Asian Chicken

6 boneless, skinless chicken breasts
1 (6-ounce) can frozen lemonade concentrate, thawed
¼ cup soy sauce
1 teaspoon minced garlic
1 teaspoon dried oregano
Black pepper, to taste

Combine all ingredients in a baking dish, coating chicken well. Bake at 400°
for 20 to 30 minutes. Makes 6 servings.

Tangy Chicken Thighs

2 pounds boneless, skinless chicken thighs, cut into 1½-inch pieces
1 (14-ounce) can tomatoes, diced and undrained
1 (6-ounce) can tomato paste
1 onion, chopped
2 cups diced carrots
1 tablespoon dried basil
1 teaspoon dried oregano
½ teaspoon dried thyme, crushed
½ teaspoon rosemary, crumbled
2 garlic cloves, crushed
½ teaspoon black pepper
½ cup fresh orange juice
1½ teaspoons sugar
2 tablespoons orange zest
2 tablespoons lemon juice
4 slices cooked bacon, crumbled

Combine first 13 ingredients and 1 tablespoon orange zest in a slow cooker
on low heat. Mix thoroughly. Cover and cook for 6 to 6½ hours, or until
chicken is cooked throughout. Stir in lemon juice and remaining orange zest.
Serve sprinkled with crumbled bacon. Makes 8 servings.

Tangy Lime Chicken

6 boneless, skinless chicken breasts
1 cup Italian dressing
Juice and zest of 2 limes
Salt and black pepper, to taste

Place chicken in large greased baking dish. Combine dressing, lime juice,
and lime zest. Season with salt and pepper. Pour mixture over chicken. Bake
at 400° for about 30 minutes. Makes 6 servings.

Taverna Chicken

1 (4-pound) chicken, cut into pieces
1 onion, chopped
2 garlic cloves, minced
1 green bell pepper, chopped
1 medium ripe tomato, peeled and chopped
1 cup chicken broth
Dash cayenne pepper

Combine all ingredients in a slow cooker. Cover and cook on low for 6 to 8 hours. Makes 8 servings.

Tennessee Breast of Chicken

4 boneless, skinless chicken breasts
¼ cup all-purpose flour
½ teaspoon paprika
Salt and black pepper, to taste
2 tablespoons butter
2 tablespoons oil
2 tablespoons chopped onion
2 tablespoons chopped parsley
¼ teaspoon dried chervil
¼ cup Dr. Pepper
1 (4-ounce) can mushrooms, undrained
1 (10-ounce) can tomatoes
¼ teaspoon sugar

Dredge chicken in flour that has been mixed with paprika, salt, and pepper. Heat butter and oil in a skillet, and sauté chicken on both sides until lightly browned. Stir in onion, parsley, and chervil, and cook briefly. Remove from heat. Place contents in a slow cooker. Combine remaining ingredients and pour over chicken. Cover and cook on low for 6 to 7 hours. Serve with noodles or rice. Makes 4 servings.

Teriyaki Chicken

6 boneless, skinless chicken breasts
1 onion, sliced
1 red bell pepper, chopped
1 (4-ounce) can sliced water chestnuts, drained
1 cup teriyaki sauce
1 (15-ounce) can pineapple chunks, drained

Combine all ingredients, coating chicken well. Bake at 400° for 20 to 30 minutes. Makes 6 servings.

Thai Cilantro Barbecue Chicken

½ cup chopped fresh cilantro
¼ cup vegetable oil
¼ cup finely sliced green onions
3 tablespoons lime juice
1 tablespoon fish sauce
1 tablespoon sugar
2 teaspoons minced garlic
2 teaspoons minced ginger
1 teaspoon hot bean paste
½ teaspoon salt
6 whole chicken legs

Combine all marinade ingredients. Place chicken in a resealable plastic bag set in a shallow dish. Pour marinade mixture over chicken; close bag. Marinate in refrigerator 2 to 4 hours, turning occasionally to distribute marinade.

Place chicken in center of cooking grate. Grill over indirect heat for 30 minutes, or until juices run clear, turning once halfway through grilling time. Makes 6 servings.

Tortilla-Crusted Chicken

1 cup finely crushed tortilla chips
½ teaspoon dried oregano, crushed
¼ teaspoon ground cumin
¼ teaspoon freshly ground black pepper
1 egg
4 boneless, skinless chicken breasts

Coat a large inch baking pan with cooking spray; set aside. In a shallow dish, combine tortilla chips, oregano, cumin, and pepper. Place egg in another shallow dish; beat slightly. Dip chicken in beaten egg, and coat with tortilla chip mixture. Arrange chicken in the prepared baking pan. Bake at 375° for about 25 minutes, or until chicken is no longer pink. Makes 4 servings.

Tropical Chicken

3 garlic cloves, minced
2 tablespoons olive oil
1 (3½-pound) whole chicken, cut into pieces
3 bay leaves
½ cup water
1 cup orange juice
2 tablespoons lime juice
2 tablespoons coarsely ground black pepper
Salt, to taste

Heat garlic in olive oil. Place chicken in the bottom of a slow cooker, and add remaining ingredients. Cover and cook on low for 8 hours. Makes 4 servings.

White Cheddar Chicken with Apple Raisin Chutney

2 tablespoons extra-virgin olive oil
8 boneless, skinless chicken breasts
1 teaspoon onion powder
1 teaspoon garlic powder
¼ teaspoon ground allspice
Salt and black pepper, to taste
8 slices white Cheddar cheese
2 large Granny Smith apples, peeled, cored, and finely chopped
½ cup golden raisins
½ cup finely minced sweet onion
¼ cup apple cider vinegar
2 tablespoons water
2 tablespoons sugar
1 tablespoon brown sugar
½ teaspoon ground cinnamon
¼ teaspoon ground allspice
¼ teaspoon ground cloves
Apple slices, for garnish
Mint sprigs, for garnish

Add olive oil to a large skillet over medium-high heat. Season chicken with mixture of onion powder, garlic powder, allspice, salt, and pepper. Add chicken to oil and cook about 3 minutes per side. Transfer chicken to a large, rimmed baking sheet. Top each chicken breast with a slice of white Cheddar cheese. Bake at 400° for 15 to 20 minutes, or until chicken is cooked through.

Meanwhile, combine the chopped apple, raisins, onion, apple cider vinegar, water, sugars, cinnamon, allspice, and cloves in a saucepan over medium-high heat. Stir to dissolve sugar. Bring to a boil, reduce heat, and cover. Simmer for 30 to 40 minutes, or until liquid has cooked off. Season to taste with salt.

Serve chicken with chutney, and garnish with apple slices and mint. Makes 8 servings.

A

365 Easy Chicken Recipes